Praise for *Making Every Geography Lesson Count*

One of the major pitfalls of implementing research-informed advice from cognitive psychology is that the subsequent strategies are often applied too generally. *Making Every Geography Lesson Count* takes a subject-specific approach, brilliantly appropriating some of the most important discoveries in the field in a concise and practical way. If I were a geography teacher, this book would be my bible.

Carl Hendrick, co-author of
What Does This Look Like in the Classroom?

In this sharp, beautifully written account of what constitutes high-quality provision and practice in the teaching of geography, Mark Enser scopes the subject's big picture – its history, narrative and fertile questions – while holding in balance the detail of the small stuff which leads to authentic learning. This is no mean feat, and *Making Every Geography Lesson Count* succeeds by cleverly interweaving into Mark's lyrical commentary some hilariously funny anecdotes and a range of classroom scenarios to lift the lid on this great subject.

If you weren't already in love with geography before reading this book, you will be by the time you finish it.

Mary Myatt, education adviser, writer and author of
Curriculum: Gallimaufry to Coherence

My own experience of geography lessons in school was one of boredom and ennui. All I can really remember is labelling drawings of blast furnaces and designing a poster about Malthus' "Four Horsemen of the Apocalypse". Needless to say, I quit the subject as soon as I could.

Reading *Making Every Geography Lesson Count*, however, fills me with regret for what might have been – as Mark Enser's deep knowledge of, and irrepressible enthusiasm for, his subject is a thing of joy. But this book is not just a treasure trove of geographical teaching tips; it is also underpinned by a finely honed understanding of how children learn and the most effective ways to help them make progress.

Put away the colouring pencils, this book has everything you need to make every geography lesson count!

David Didau, author of *Making Kids Cleverer*

In *Making Every Geography Lesson Count* Mark Enser provides a valuable addition to an already fantastic series. Two things in particular radiate from the book. First, it becomes evident very quickly that Mark is a fully committed subject practitioner: he says at one point that "passion is contagious", and this comes across in every case study and example he shares. Second, he is as well-versed in current pedagogical thinking as any teacher could wish to be. Whether it's using examples from Rosenshine and the EEF, or delving into metacognition and self-regulation, he's got every base covered as he synthesises theory and practice into a text that is inspiring, practical and very readable.

Making Every Geography Lesson Count will breathe confidence into every geography teacher that reads it.

Robin Macpherson, Assistant Rector, Dollar Academy

If only I had been able to read *Making Every Geography Lesson Count* when I started out as a geography teacher. I'm sure it would been thumbed to bits by now. Mark Enser's love of geography shines through this remarkable book as he thoughtfully combines his subject knowledge and deep pedagogical understanding with the seminal work of the likes of Daniel Willingham, Rob Coe, Barak Rosenshine and, of course, Shaun Allison and Andy Tharby. The result is a very well structured, beautifully exemplified and helpfully challenging book brimming with practical strategies for teachers to consider.

Making Every Geography Lesson Count is a must-read for any geography teacher, experienced or novice, as well for those charged with training our next generation of teachers.

**Andy Buck, CEO, Leadership Matters,
Honorary Vice President, Geographical Association**

Making every
geography
lesson count

Six principles to support
great geography teaching

Mark Enser

Edited by Shaun Allison and Andy Tharby

Crown House Publishing Limited
www.crownhouse.co.uk

First published by

Crown House Publishing Limited
Crown Buildings, Bancyfelin, Carmarthen, Wales, SA33 5ND, UK
www.crownhouse.co.uk

and

Crown House Publishing Company LLC
PO Box 2223, Williston, VT 05495, USA
www.crownhousepublishing.com

First published 2019. Reprinted 2019.

British Library Cataloguing-in-Publication Data

A catalogue entry for this book is available from the British Library.

Print ISBN 978-178583339-7
Mobi ISBN 978-178583403-5
ePub ISBN 978-178583404-2
ePDF ISBN 978-178583405-9

LCCN 2018961970

Printed and bound in the UK by

TJ International, Padstow, Cornwall

Foreword

When Andy Tharby and I wrote *Making Every Lesson Count* we were quite clear about what we wanted to achieve. A book that would bridge the gap between educational research and day-to-day classroom practice. We had both become tired of the endless stream of fads and gimmicks that had permeated education, from brain gym to learning styles and triple-impact marking and beyond. We just wanted a simple answer to a simple question: "What does great teaching look like?"

So this is what we set about doing. We spent a great deal of time reading educational books, blogs and research papers about what seemed to work in teaching. At the same time we talked to some of the very best teachers we knew about what they did, day in and day out, that appeared to result in them getting the most fantastic outcomes with the young people they taught. After a while it became clear to us that great teaching could be distilled into six key principles:

- ♦ Challenge – the best teachers have the very highest expectations of all of the students they teach.

- ♦ Explanation – the best teachers are brilliant at explaining really tricky ideas clearly and with confidence.

- ♦ Modelling – the best teachers understand the importance of "walking" their students through what to do with their acquired knowledge and skills.

- ♦ Practice – the best teachers know that in order to learn something, students have to practise with purpose.

- ♦ Feedback – the best teachers give accurate and timely feedback to make their students think about what they are learning.

- ♦ Questioning – the best teachers know how to ask really good questions to get their students thinking.

And so *Making Every Lesson Count* was born! A practical book for busy teachers who want to know how to translate the best available research evidence into their classrooms. As we trawled through the many teacher bloggers who were doing this and writing about it, we became aware of Mark Enser. Mark was head of geography at a school not far from us in East Sussex. Through reading his blogs, it became very clear to us that Mark's view on teaching was very close to our own. He writes in his blog:

> "It may be true to claim that 'everything works somewhere' but that isn't especially relevant. What we need to know is what is most likely to work most of the time. We need to look not just at what will work, but what will work best, as in both most effective and most efficient. There is no point in an approach to teaching that requires 25 hours a day and 8 days a week ... Teaching does not need to be complicated. We need to reclaim our profession and start to teach like nobody's watching." [1]

For too long, too many teachers have been expected to teach in a way that has no evidence behind it. As Mark suggests, surely a more sensible approach is to use the research evidence that exists to shape what we do. Not only is this important from a teacher workload point of view, but also for our students from a moral purpose point of view. The education of our young people is too important to be left to chance. We owe it to them to base our teaching on what is most likely to work. While research evidence cannot provide us with all the answers, it can certainly guide us in the right direction and help us avoid pedagogical dead ends and wrong turns.

So when we decided to commission subject-specific versions of *Making Every Lesson Count*, Mark was the obvious choice to write the geography version. He is incredibly passionate about his subject, remarkably knowledgeable about educational research and has a great talent for communicating this in a way that makes sense to busy teachers. With this in mind, it comes as no surprise that what he has produced with *Making Every Geography Lesson Count* is an invaluable guide for geography teachers everywhere.

We hope that you enjoy it and that it gives you the confidence to "teach like nobody's watching".

Shaun Allison

---

1 Mark Enser, Teach Like Nobody's Watching, *Teaching It Real* [blog] (12 September 2018). Available at: https://teachreal.wordpress.com/2018/09/12/teach-like-nobodys-watching-2/.

Acknowledgements

I need to thank Shaun Allison and Andy Tharby for writing the original book that began this series. Reading *Making Every Lesson Count* in 2015 helped to change my perspective on teaching and revealed a different way to see what was happening in the classroom.

I also need to thank my amazing geography department colleagues at Heathfield Community College – Rob Messetter, Sian Parker and Karen Amer – whose excellent practice permeates this book. The wider geography colleagues found on social media have also been instrumental in helping to form these ideas. A huge thank you to each and every brilliant #geographyteacher on Twitter.

Finally, I'd like to thank my wife, Zoe, the most inspirational teacher I know, for her support, patience and expertise.

Contents

Introduction

How Do We Make Every Geography Lesson Count?

Teaching, at its heart, is quite simple. We pick something we want students to learn, we talk to them about it and we give them some activities to do. Then we see how much they have learnt and give them some feedback on it. Behind this simplicity, however, is a lot more complexity, including some difficult questions:

♦ What do we want students to learn?

♦ How can we make sure that they remember what we say about it?

♦ Which activities will help them to learn what we want them to learn?

♦ How do we find out what they have learnt?

♦ What kind of feedback will be most effective?

It is questions like these that Shaun Allison and Andy Tharby's *Making Every Lesson Count* sought to answer and that this book goes on to explore in the context of the geography classroom.[1]

---

1 Shaun Allison and Andy Tharby, *Making Every Lesson Count: Six Principles to Support Great Teaching and Learning* (Carmarthen: Crown House Publishing, 2015).

The need for subject-specific approaches to pedagogy is very clear. While there are many common threads to excellent teaching – shown through the six principles for effective teaching and learning in *Making Every Lesson Count*, see page 3 – the geography classroom is a very different place to the maths or history classroom. Our curriculum is structured differently, we explain things geographically, we model uniquely geographical things and we ask questions as geographers. The way in which we make a geography lesson count will be different to how we approach a history lesson or a maths lesson; hence the need for this series of books.

Before we can delve into how to make our lessons count, we first need to agree on the purpose of a lesson. If we think it is to develop a student's character or to prepare them with twenty-first-century life skills then our priorities and methods might be different. However, I am working on the basis that, fundamentally, we want students to learn geography. We want them to leave the room with an improved knowledge of the world, a better understanding of how it works and the geographical skills to support their understanding.

By putting "learn geography" as the core purpose of the lesson, we draw on several underpinning ideas from educational research. To learn geography, students need to spend time thinking about the content, so that they are then able to remember it. The first insight is from Kirschner, Sweller and Clark, who state that "learning, in turn, is defined as a

Expert teaching requires …
Challenge
So that …
Students have high expectations of what they can achieve
Explanation
So that …
Students acquire new knowledge and skills
Modelling
So that …
Students know how to apply the knowledge and skills
Students engage in deliberate practice
Questioning
So that …
Students are made to think hard with breadth, depth and accuracy
Feedback
So that …
Students think about and further develop their knowledge and skills

Scaffolding

change in long-term memory".[2] We can add to this the idea from Daniel T. Willingham, who argues that "memory is the residue of thought".[3] If we want to remember something, we need to think about that thing. Putting these two ideas together, we can see that for us to claim that learning has happened, students need to have relevant information to hand in their long-term memory – and for it to get there they need to have thought hard about it.

We know that in order for students to be able to recall information from their long-term memory it helps to have practised retrieving this information a lot, by bringing it to mind on a regular basis.[4]

The reason why we want this information to be readily available is because having to look something up every time we want to use it will overly tax working memory. For example, we could, in theory, not commit what a meander is to memory. Instead we could look up the word when we wanted to use it (assuming we knew what to search for), but then we might also need to look up thalweg, helicoidal flow, slip-off slope and hydraulic action. We would need to keep all these new definitions and pieces of information in our working memory before we could use them to describe what was happening on a bend in a river. Far better to know what these things are so we can focus on doing something with this information.

---

2   Paul A. Kirschner, John Sweller and Richard E. Clark, Why Minimal Guidance during Instruction Does Not Work: An Analysis of the Failure of Constructivist, Discovery, Project-Based, Experiential, and Inquiry-Based Teaching, *Educational Psychologist* 41(2) (2006): 75–86 at 75.

3   Daniel T. Willingham, *Why Don't Students Like School? A Cognitive Scientist Answers Questions About How the Mind Works and What It Means for the Classroom* (San Francisco, CA: Jossey-Bass, 2009), p. 54.

4   Benjamin C. Storm, Robert A. Bjork and Jennifer C. Storm, Optimizing Retrieval as a Learning Event: When and Why Expanding Retrieval Practice Enhances Long-Term Retention, *Memory and Cognition*, 38(2) (2010): 244–253.

These ideas on memory and learning sit at the heart of this book, alongside the curriculum; the things that we want students to remember. We will explore both what we want students to learn, and how we can use insights from research to increase the likelihood of them committing this content to memory. Each chapter looks at one of the six principles, first outlined in *Making Every Lesson Count*, discussing the underpinning theory and then offering practical strategies for bringing this into the geography classroom. Each chapter ends with a case study from a fellow geography teacher who has successfully employed the principle in their own classroom.

The first principle of *challenge* argues that we need to understand what we mean by progress in geography so that we can ensure our lessons stretch all students. This chapter asks that we set the bar high but then suggests strategies to ensure that all students can reach this level. It also discusses the idea of using threshold concepts and fertile questions to help plan a curriculum.

Challenge naturally leads on to the second principle, *explanation*. To challenge students to think hard about geography we need to explain geographical ideas clearly and in a way that makes them memorable. This chapter suggests that we can do this through the use of analogies, stories and well-chosen case studies, and by implementing the principles of dual coding to support working memory.

As well as explaining what we need students to understand, we want to *model* what it is we want them to be able to do. This is our third principle. This chapter discusses what we model and how to do so in a way that supports students in applying it to their work. It also suggests how we can gradually remove this scaffolding to end up with independent learners.

All of this is done to allow the fourth principle, *practice*, to take place. This chapter returns to the idea of the curriculum sitting at the heart of the lesson and the use of retrieval practice to make sure that the curriculum's content is actually learnt, and can be recalled and used when needed. It also considers the role of enquiry in the geography classroom and how the independent investigation at A level can be used to structure the practice of guided enquiry from Key Stage 3.

The fifth principle, *feedback*, is a part of the learning process that, when done inefficiently, can dominate a teacher's time at the expense of everything else. This chapter shows how, while feedback is a vital part of learning, it doesn't need to take the form of time-consuming written comments in books and could instead be done verbally as part of every lesson.

The final principle, *questioning*, is critical to effective teaching. This chapter asks how we can create a culture in which students are happy to ask and answer questions and how we can use high-quality, subject-specific questioning to create the next generation of geographers.

The conclusion considers how these six principles can be pulled together in the classroom. We want to avoid seeing each principle as being a distinct "bit" of the lesson: I am now doing explanation, then I will stop and do questioning, next is the modelling part. Instead we should consider how these aspects intertwine to create an approach to teaching effectively and efficiently.

While this book contains clear strategies that we can use in the classroom to make every lesson count, it doesn't contain any silver bullets. Too many problems in our schools have been created by people claiming that we all need to use a particular method in a particular way to get results. Instead, this book, like the others in the series, is concerned more with sharing *why* certain things may be more effective than with directing you towards *what* you should do with the information. Only the individual teacher will be able to judge what they think is best for their class, but being mindful of research to inform our decision-making can only be a good thing.

Geography is an exciting subject with a history going back millennia to Eratosthenes, who first coined the term *geögraphia*, literally meaning "writing the world". When we teach geography, we are looking back through thousands of years of discoveries about our planet and are passing on what has been learnt to the next generation. This geographical education is giving them the key to their planet, to their inheritance. It is a huge responsibility and honour with which to be entrusted. Let's find a way to make it count.

Chapter 1

Challenge

Katie

Katie arrives at her first A level geography lesson and feels a sense of déjà vu. On the board is a picture of Old Harry Rocks with the word "Coasts!" displayed enthusiastically above it. "I bet we're looking at longshore drift," she thinks as she slumps into her seat. She remembers looking at this last spring when revising for her GCSE, and a year ago for her controlled assessment and doing a project on it in Year 8, as well as in Year 6. She finds it hard to remember a time when she didn't know how waves move sediment along the coast.

Tom

Tom is sat in his A level geography class feeling lost, again. The teacher is asking how a lack of longshore drift helps to explain why geographers now think that Chesil Beach was formed as an offshore bar brought on land during sea level changes. Tom doesn't know. He is still trying to figure out where coastal sediment comes from in the first place.

In order to think about how we plan a challenging geography lesson we need to understand the nature of progress in the discipline. This can be difficult in a knowledge- and content-heavy subject like ours, in which it can, at times, feel as though the curriculum is made up of distinct topics – silos of information – that have little in common with each other. This can lead to it seeming like students are making little progression over the year other than in terms of an accumulation of information about these disparate topics; but as we know, learning facts about coasts doesn't necessarily lead to you being a better geographer when you learn about urbanisation.

However, the accumulation of information on a diverse range of topics is of vital importance in building an understanding of geography. Without first gaining this knowledge, we can't start to put it together in order to see the connections. It might be that we just need to change our timescale when we think about progress in our subject and, instead of asking "What progress should students make this term?", ask "What progress should they make between different key stages?" If we compare the work we ask students to do in Year 7 and the work we ask them to do in Year 13 we get a better sense of what progression, and therefore challenge, looks like in geography.

Liz Taylor suggests that progression in geography has certain characteristics.[1] It means that students develop a broader and deeper knowledge: broader meaning that they

1   Liz Taylor, Progression. In Mark Jones (ed.), *The Handbook of Secondary Geography* (Sheffield: Geographical Association, 2017), pp. 40–47.

study more topics and depth referring to the level of sophistication with which they can express ideas about them. They move from concrete examples – such as the distribution of houses in our local community – to theoretical understandings – such as the Burgess model of land use. They progress from studying things at a local to a global scale, they develop an ability to see the links between topics – that synoptic approach of combining different silos of information together – and they acquire a greater range of skills and a greater independence in knowing when to deploy these skills.

This gives us a good starting point in considering what it means to make a geography lesson challenging. We want to not only increase their knowledge of a range of topics but also ensure that they know these topics in enough depth to reach sophisticated conclusions and do this on a range of scales – local, regional, national and international. We want to make sure that they are moving beyond their own experiences and are able to apply theoretical models to a range of places. As such, we will need to ensure that they are equipped with a well-developed toolbox of geographical skills to deploy to this end.

We can see the nature of progression most clearly if we look at a topic that students study at a range of key stages, such as the workings of ecosystems. In the national curriculum for Key Stage 3, students are expected to look at the physical characteristics of different regions of the world. This might mean that they learn about the basic structures of the ecosystem in a given area – the food web, the nutrient cycle and so on – and about how human activity can affect these structures. The focus is typically more localised and there is less emphasis on drawing wider conclusions about the way in which *all* ecosystems work.

By the time they get to Key Stage 4, students will need to be able to contrast different ecosystems – such as those in the tropics and those in deserts – and to understand the factors that influence the nutrient cycle in these different conditions. They will also need to draw on more detailed examples of the opportunities for economic development offered by these ecosystems, and of the challenges they present. Students will need to hone the ability to apply these ideas in different and unfamiliar situations.

In Key Stage 5, the focus narrows to look at how the water and carbon cycles operate in these ecosystems, with a need to appreciate more fully the ways in which flows and stores act and are acted upon. Students are expected to be able to discuss in some depth the management strategies used to tackle changes in these two earth life support systems and evaluate their impact.

By looking at the curriculum in this way we can get a better appreciation of what "challenging" geography might look like at different points. This then suggests ways in which we can create schemes of work that build not only over a particular topic but also between key stages.

The following strategies suggest ways in which you can put this challenge at the heart of each of your lessons.

1. Know Thy Subject

What do we need to know before we begin?

In *What Makes Great Teaching?*, Professor Robert Coe et al. identify and analyse the features of effective classroom practice. On a teacher's subject knowledge, they write:

---

1. (Pedagogical) content knowledge (Strong evidence of impact on student outcomes)

The most effective teachers have deep knowledge of the subjects they teach, and when teachers' knowledge falls below a certain level it is a significant impediment to students' learning. As well as a strong understanding of the material being taught, teachers must also understand the ways students think about the content, be able to evaluate the thinking behind students' own methods, and identify students' common misconceptions.[2]

Of all the factors analysed, only effective instruction was found to be as important, with similarly strong evidence on student outcomes. There was less evidence in support of the impact of the following features of classroom practice:[3]

- ◆ Classroom climate (Moderate evidence of impact on student outcomes).

- ◆ Classroom management (Moderate evidence of impact on student outcomes).

- ◆ Teacher beliefs (Some evidence of impact on student outcomes).

- ◆ Professional behaviours (Some evidence of impact on student outcomes).

Despite this, a lot of initial teacher training and continuing professional development (CPD) focuses more on these less significant elements, with almost no time given to developing subject knowledge itself. In response to this concern many schools have started handing CPD time back to departments. While this is a great start, it doesn't automatically mean that there will be more time spent on subject knowledge. A huge amount of departmental CPD involves planning schemes of work, developing assessments and, sadly, administration tasks. There needs to be a real change in school culture to recognise the importance of teachers staying on top of their subject knowledge. Once we accept

---

2   Robert Coe et al., *What Makes Great Teaching? Review of the Underpinning Research* (London: Sutton Trust, 2014). Available at: https://www.suttontrust.com/wp-content/uploads/2014/10/What-Makes-Great-Teaching-REPORT.pdf, p. 2.

3   Coe et al., *What Makes Great Teaching?*, p. 3.

the value of this, there are a few things we can do in practice.

First, talk to your head of department about carrying out an honest subject-knowledge audit as a team. Remember that it is human nature to overestimate our abilities, so test your department's by completing A level exam papers and checking each other's work, looking at your responses against the mark scheme. Once we are aware of the gaps in our collective knowledge we can ask to set aside time in department meetings to address them. This could involve teaching each other. Learn from each other's strengths and pool your understanding. In a department meeting, you could each teach a five-minute mini-lesson about a concept that you have been focusing on. In my school, we use this approach to cover new content when exam specifications inevitably change.

If we don't have the expertise in the department then we need to look outside it. My school is part of a subject hub for local schools, meaning we can share the cost of bringing in subject-specific CPD training sessions. If your school does not already have these kinds of links, you could investigate the feasibility of setting them up. This usually works best if there is a local network of schools who share INSET days. In terms of finding specialists to deliver training, the Geographical Association is a good place to start looking for experts.[4]

Alternatively, there are some excellent articles in *Teaching Geography*, the journal of the Geographical Association, which you could share and discuss as a department. For example, we recently explored one particularly interesting article on the science of plate tectonics, which addressed the misconceptions that are often taught, and believed, by teachers.[5] Taking time in departmental meetings to read and discuss these articles, including ideas for building the

---

4   See https://www.geography.org.uk/.
5   Duncan Hawley, On Shaky Ground: The Physical Facts of Recent Earthquake Events in Mexico, *Teaching Geography* 48(1) (2018): 32–35.

information gleaned into existing lessons, is a valuable investment.

2. Agree Excellence

How do we know what challenging work looks like?

Before we can increase the level of challenge in our class-room we have to decide what challenging geography work looks like; we need to set the bar. This can be difficult in a subject like ours. It is a very broad discipline which requires students to draw on a combination of different types of knowledge. Propositional knowledge involves understanding theoretical concepts – for example, the Bradshaw model, which shows how a river changes as it moves downstream, or the Burgess model of housing patterns – contextual knowledge requires the application of these theories to a place, and procedural knowledge involves having the skills and judgement to apply the one to the other.[6]

In our geography department at Heathfield Community College, we started our process of setting the bar by listing the key strands that are essential to success in our discipline. We came up with the following:

♦ Cartographic skills.

♦ Graphical skills.

♦ Synoptic skills.

♦ Knowledge of place.

♦ Knowledge of physical processes.

---

6 For more on how these different forms of knowledge allow us to build a geography curriculum, see: Alex Standish, The Place of Regional Geography. In Mark Jones and David Lambert (eds), *Debates in Geography Education*, 2nd edn (Abingdon: Routledge, 2018), pp. 62–74.

- ◆ Knowledge of human processes.
- ◆ The ability to use the views of stakeholders.
- ◆ Investigative skills.
- ◆ The ability to reach conclusions.

Once you have a list of these key attributes you can then start thinking about what excellence looks like for each one. Picture a top student at the end of a key stage and ask yourself, "What can they do that sets them apart?" Turn this into a short sentence that clearly explains what you are looking for in your students.

For cartographic skills at the end of GCSE:

> *"We expect an excellent geographer to be able to use maps to locate places and describe their location. We expect that they will be able to use evidence on a map to make judgements about a place and as part of decision-making exercises."*

For reaching conclusions:

> *"We expect an excellent geographer to be able to reach fully substantiated conclusions relevant to the place studied and based on the evidence gathered. They should be able to suggest further opportunities for research and be able to evaluate their conclusion to check for validity and reliability."*

These statements can be used to create exemplar pieces of work (see Chapter 3 for more on this) and as a constant reminder of your expectations.

3. Plan Across Key Stages

How does geography get more difficult?

As mentioned in the introduction to this chapter, a useful approach to challenge is to think of geography across the key stages. As the subject progresses it becomes more challenging: concepts become more advanced, case studies are used in greater depth, there is more reliance on statistical skills, and links are made between a greater number of different aspects of the subject. To increase the level of challenge in our lessons we can look ahead through the key stages and think about how we might get ahead of the game by developing these higher-level skills further down the school.

One way to achieve this is to review the topics being covered at A level and look for opportunities to build them into the GCSE course, or for the key ideas to be introduced at Key Stage 3. There are some great opportunities to do this when studying earth's life support systems in Key Stage 5. This topic focuses heavily on how negative feedback loops work to bring systems back into equilibrium; for example, if volcanic eruptions release carbon from the geosphere into the atmosphere, the plants in the biosphere utilise this carbon more quickly and draw it back out (a process known as carbon fertilisation). It also considers how human action can create positive feedback loops that amplify a particular change, such as global warming thawing permafrost, which releases more methane, which leads to increased global warming and so on. These ideas could easily be introduced into the study of ecosystems at GCSE. While this isn't strictly necessary if your aim is just to cover the specification, it will lead to a greater conceptual understanding of the subject and will help students to make sense of the content that they do need to study at that stage.

Another opportunity to draw on the increased level of challenge found later on in the subject would be to consider the independent investigation completed at the end of Key Stage 5. Challenge lies not just in the deepening subject knowledge that students will need as they progress through the key stages, but in the skills that they will need to utilise. This investigation is, in many ways, the culmination of thirteen years of geographical study. It requires that students set their own question, carry out a literature review, plan and execute their own data collection, analyse their data using tests of statistical significance where relevant, use this data to reach a conclusion and carry out a detailed evaluation of reliability and validity. There is a high level of challenge present here.

It would be too much to expect a Key Stage 3 student to carry out this kind of investigation with such a degree of independence, but a guided enquiry that follows a similar process should certainly be possible.[7] This could be a great opportunity to apply what has been learnt in a unit of work and to put the theory to the test. Simple enquiry questions could include:

---

7   For more on how such a guided enquiry could work, see: Margaret Roberts, Planning for Enquiry. In Mark Jones (ed.), *The Handbook of Secondary Geography* (Sheffield: The Geographical Association, 2017), pp. 48–60.

- Is wind direction the most important factor in determining temperature?

- How does the level of human interference affect biodiversity?

- How does residency time affect perception of a place?

- What impact does traffic congestion have on air quality?

- Which factors affect water infiltration rates?

Scaffolding needs to be deployed carefully to ensure that the level of challenge doesn't leave any student behind. This can be done through careful modelling and by leaving worked examples with some students so that they can refer to these as they practise. It can also be helpful to leave mini-whiteboards on particular students' tables so that you can quickly add sentence starters, key words or a brief paragraph structure for them to use, if you think they'd benefit from this support.

We need to be wary of seeing the curriculum as some kind of race to the end which provides students with only a shallow understanding of the topic. We need to work slowly and methodically through this challenging work, with plenty of opportunities to check for understanding and to adapt what we are doing if students seem to be struggling to keep up with our expectations. True, our expectations must be high, but we must also offer the support to ensure that students can meet them. Many of the strategies discussed in this book are designed to do just that; to ensure that all students receive an excellent geographical education.

By looking at our subject across the years we get a better sense of what we mean by "challenging geography" and can start to see how some of this challenge can be brought down to students in earlier years. The goal is to prepare students for the extended challenge that they will face in the subject, as well as to use challenge to develop a deeper understanding now.

4. Pose Fertile Questions

What do we want our students to understand?

For learning to be effective, we want to break it into small, manageable pieces that students can practise and improve upon (see Chapter 4 for more on practice). This might mean that students spend some time learning a particular compartmentalised piece of knowledge or skill – for example, to interpret a climate graph, to understand how development indicators can be used to reach conclusions about a country, about the role of mountains in creating relief rainfall or the definition of sustainable development. The problem with this approach is that we risk students seeing each skill or piece of knowledge in isolation, divorced from the rest of the discipline and outside the network of links that exist between different parts of the domain that we call the "schema". These complex links enable us to see the world geographically. When we look at a mountain range and a climate graph, we are able to make the connection between the two pieces of information. Our knowledge of the specific place allows us to make inferences about the impact of the climate. This couldn't happen if we held each piece of information in its own silo.

A better, and more challenging, approach would be to pose what Oliver Knight and David Benson term a "fertile question". They explain the concept by saying it is "a planning device for knitting together a sequence of lessons, so that all of the learning activities … move towards the resolution of an interesting problem by means of a substantial motivating activity at the end."[8] This idea could be tailor-made for geography, as the solving of real-world problems sits at the heart of the subject. One example could be "Should the Lesotho Highland Water Project have been built?" The problem-solving activities would involve students: contrasting the climate graphs for Lesotho and the Gauteng province in South Africa, and studying the effects of the Drakensberg mountains on the amount of rainfall; comparing the development data with the relative water needs of the two areas; and studying the nature of the project itself, applying the concept of sustainability.

Other fertile questions could include:

♦ What impact did the Alaskan oil pipeline have on the carbon and water cycle?

♦ Can intermediate technology solve the water crisis?

♦ Should London become the first urban national park?

♦ Did aid make the effects of Haiti's earthquake worse?

♦ Can tropical rainforests be exploited in a sustainable way?

These fertile questions then become the starting point for planning a sequence of lessons, structuring in curricular content and opportunities to develop necessary skills. For example, the question on London becoming the world's first urban national park would fit well into a GCSE topic on the

---

8   Oliver Knight and David Benson, *Creating Outstanding Classrooms: A Whole-School Approach* (Abingdon: Routledge, 2014), p. 74.

urban environment. It would allow students to look at the priorities for urban areas in high-income countries, with a particular focus on whether green space should be protected or developed. Broad and open-ended questions allow students to really stretch their own thinking and understanding.

This approach involves combining small steps of deliberate practice that lead to secure learning with the more challenging step of applying what students have learnt to a real context. By regularly using targeted fertile questions, it also means that we revisit key threshold concepts like sustainability and development often, and this recall can strengthen the retention of information.[9]

5. Cross the Threshold

What do students need to know before they can move on?

If we look back to Tom's experience at the beginning of the chapter, we can see one barrier to setting challenging questions in geography; they are inevitably based on a huge amount of prior knowledge. Let's unpick this question:

How does a lack of longshore drift help to explain why geographers now think that Chesil Beach was formed as an offshore bar brought on land during sea level changes?

To answer this question fully you would need to know:

♦ What longshore drift is and how it operates.

---

9 A huge amount has been written about retrieval practice and its role in memory. A good starting point is Henry L. Roediger and Andrew C. Butler, The Critical Role of Retrieval Practice in Long-Term Retention, *Trends in Cognitive Sciences* 15(1) (2011): 20–27.

- What an offshore bar is.

- How offshore bars form.

- That sea levels have changed over time.

- The specific details about this area of coast.

If Tom missed a lesson on longshore drift in Year 7, he might never be able to answer this question for himself, unless we are able to realise that he has this fundamental gap in his knowledge. The idea that particular knowledge is key to student progress was developed by economics lecturers Jan Mayer and Ray Land, who noticed that their students seemed to be blocked by the same recurring barriers. They identified certain ideas that were so fundamental to their subject that students were unable to make progress if they were not secure in their understanding of them. They termed these ideas "threshold concepts" and suggested that they are:[10]

- **Transformative:** they change the way in which you see the world.

- **Troublesome:** they might seem counterintuitive or alien.

- **Irreversible:** the transformative nature means that once they are learnt, the concepts are unlikely to be forgotten.

- **Integrated:** they reveal connections between the different parts of the discipline.

- **Bounded:** despite this integration, these concepts only apply within defined parameters.

- **Discursive:** they lead to the development of new language.

---

10 Jan H. F. Meyer and Ray Land, Threshold Concepts and Troublesome Knowledge: Linkages to Ways of Thinking and Practising within the Disciplines. In Chris Rust (ed.), *Improving Student Learning: Theory and Practice Ten Years On* (Oxford: Oxford Centre for Staff and Learning Development, 2003), pp. 412–424.

We work with these threshold concepts all the time in geography. I'd suggest that longshore drift is one of them as it changes the way in which you see the coast and without it you can't understand other parts of the topic, such as coastal management.

Another threshold concept that students struggle with in geography is seeing the world as a three-dimensional sphere. They are so used to seeing the world represented as two-dimensional map projections – often from the same perspective with the Greenwich meridian at the centre – that they struggle to make sense of other representations of the planet. This often leads to confusion about the proximity of Russia to the USA or about the vast distances between islands in the South Pacific. Without this conceptual schema they will struggle to understand elements of plate tectonics, trade routes and trading blocs, longitude and latitude and climate. This threshold concept needs to be secure before they can move on. In this example, we can achieve this through exposing students to an array of different representations of the world in different lessons and activities. Avoid always falling back on a Mercator projection map with the Prime Meridian running through the centre.

Once we have identified threshold concepts in our schemes of work there is a lot we can do to ensure that students have frequent opportunities to explore them:

- **Use them to help structure our program of study.** Geography lends itself to the idea of a spiral curriculum. We can make sure that threshold concepts are taught early, taught well and revisited often.

- **Use them when planning a sequence of learning.** Are you introducing these threshold concepts at the start of the topic?

- **Plan to test these concepts.** We need to make sure that students are secure in this threshold knowledge before moving on, so we need to identify who has gaps and where. (See Chapter 5 for ideas.)

- **Close these gaps.** If students haven't grasped these threshold concepts then there is no point in moving on regardless. We need to plan activities to help them fill in these gaps. One simple way to do this is to test their knowledge with a quick five-question quiz. For each question, add an activity that they need to complete if they get the answer wrong. For example, if they haven't grasped the implications of the earth as a globe, have them measure the shortest route between five places. Make sure this involves doing things like travelling over the arctic circle or across the Pacific.

- **Revisit often.** We need to plan to link new information back to these threshold concepts to demonstrate the links between different parts of the discipline. Use fertile questions to give students the chance to explore these concepts in different contexts.

By first focusing our attention on securing these threshold concepts, we can then move on to challenging questions, knowing that our students have the knowledge and understanding to tackle them.

6. Wider Engagement

How can we get students exploring the subject themselves?

A final strategy for improving challenge in the lesson is to look beyond it. Geography is all around us and we can help our students to seize the opportunity to see this.

One idea is to use a blog to share different news articles.[11] This gives us the opportunity to add a brief commentary to each piece to help make it more accessible for the students – they might lack the contextual knowledge to make sense of it otherwise – and to include some prompt questions for them to consider when reading it. This is a quick way to encourage students to take an interest in the world around them and to become more knowledgeable about world events. I also make sure that there are geographical books available in the classroom for students to borrow, and that I frequently talk about what I am reading. We need to show students what resources are out there and we need to make them accessible.

We can also look to bring in experts to talk to students about their work. Local Geographical Association groups often host talks that are open to sixth form students, and universities are always keen to reach out to local schools. It is worth keeping in touch with your own university alumni, some of whom may have gone on to be successful geographers.

We can also use fieldwork to go beyond the classroom experience. This could involve taking students out of school to

---

11 My department's can be found at https://geographyexcel.wordpress.com/.

collect data as part of an investigation or we could conduct this around the school site. It is also possible to set data collection as part of a homework task, the results of which will then be used in lessons. This could take various forms: taking photographs to illustrate key ideas – such as evidence of succession in overgrown urban areas, the impact of microclimate on frost formation, or different land uses on the journey to school; conducting questionnaires; or collecting observational traffic or footfall data, for example.

The difficulty with these types of extracurricular engagements is in making sure that all students, or at least as many students as possible, can access them – and choose to do so. We can try to make sure that they *can* access them by keeping things low-cost and making sure that we have spare equipment and resources to lend them – for example, cameras, clinometers, pH testing kits, and so on. I'd suggest becoming very friendly with the science technicians!

We can also make it more likely that pupils will *choose* to engage with these activities by exploiting the fact that geography is a naturally fascinating subject which resonates with their existing interests and, more importantly, their curiosity. We could also offer incentives. Some schools offer a range of activities as part of their "super curriculum" – which is a curriculum that goes above and beyond what is offered in class but is still linked to a specific subject – and the chance to gain reward points or be entered into prize draws to those taking part.

Case Study: Challenge

Jen Monk, head of geography, Golborne High School

I think that we, as a department, have really increased the challenge in our lessons; however, I found that homework and supplementary work often lacked challenge, as rarely did it expand students' learning. I felt we were missing a trick. After trying a few different ideas, I created some extension tasks that could help students who wanted to do additional work on a topic they found hard, who wanted to push themselves further outside of the content we study in lessons or who were just really interested in a specific topic. I think we all have lots of students in our classrooms who fit these categories, but they don't necessarily want to ask for extra work.

Getting students to complete these optional tasks is linked to the idea of challenge and reward, but it also helps to identify the type of tasks that will interest them. I often find that boys don't like the idea of reading, and therefore giving them the more enjoyable option of watching documentaries or making notes helps encourage completion. I vary these optional tasks and give students links to YouTube videos or documentaries, various exam questions to answer, an additional case study to research, links to articles to read or podcasts to listen to, for instance. We have a reward system in our department whereby students who go above and beyond receive a raffle ticket and have the chance to win a half-termly prize. It seemed a good idea to award raffle tickets to further incentivise completion of these tasks; students provide evidence that they have furthered their own learning and, in return, we award them their ticket.

Chapter 2
Explanation

Michael

Michael, a geography NQT, has just got back from a training course on which he was reminded that students only remember 5% of what they are told but 90% of what they find out for themselves. He throws away his carefully structured lesson on the Boscastle floods and instead books a computer room so students can research the causes of the flood themselves. At the end of the lesson he takes a look at the summaries of their findings. Some have copied and pasted the Wikipedia entry on the topic, others have said little more than "it rained a lot". "What went wrong?" he wonders.

Sarah

Sarah is sat in Mr Smith's geography class listening to him talk about the Boscastle floods as he paces the room. He has spoken about the physical causes, made the class giggle at the name of the hill Brown Willy, talked about how the

management of the drainage basin may have made things
more severe, described the impact and told them how different
people responded, all in a huge amount of detail. It was really
interesting. "Right," he says, "use what I have told you to write
a report about the floods in Boscastle." Sarah looks at her
blank page. She thinks she remembers something about heavy
rain.

Good-quality explanation sits at the heart of what we do in
geography. As we know from Coe et al., alongside subject
knowledge, and closely tied to it, nothing has quite so much
impact as quality instruction.[1] Yet this is something that has
become contentious in recent years.

One reason for the contention over teacher explanation
stems from Edgar Dale's cone of experience, also known as
the "learning pyramid".[2] This is a theoretical, pseudo-
scientific visual framework that has morphed into several
enduring myths about learning. Most teachers will have
been given information which is apparently based on this
work – for example, that students only remember 5% of
what they are told but 90% of what they teach others.

There is not – and never has been – any evidence to support
these claims and yet they still appear in CPD sessions and in
literature for teachers. Even now the fault in the original
idea is well-known, it is so deeply ingrained as "good practice" that it still holds sway; I've met plenty of teachers who
limit how much time they spend talking to classes as a
result.

The problem with trying to explain less and instead give
students more time to discover things for themselves is that
geography is a vast and complex subject. You could spend a
lifetime staring at a cliff face without being able to identify

---

1   Coe et al., *What Makes Great Teaching?*, p. 2.
2   See, for example, Emma Jones, Cone of Experience by Edgar Dale,
    E-Learning Network [blog] (8 February 2018). Available at: http://resources.
    eln.io/experiences-cone-dale/.

for yourself how exfoliation leads to weathering or how the algae on the wave-cut platform is causing increased carbonation.

The world is a vast place and our explanation can make it come alive in our classrooms. It would be wonderful if our students could travel to the rainforest and investigate for themselves how the nutrient cycle operates there but this simply isn't practical for a whole host of reasons. Our collective understanding of the world as we now know it has been cultivated through a process of discovery that has taken humanity tens of thousands of years. Our students can't just happen upon an understanding of everything the world has to offer; we need to provide the shortcut to the best of what is known and has been discovered. We need to share the intellectual legacy of our subject. Our job as geography specialists is to provide the link between the canon of knowledge about our subject and our students. As such, we are the most powerful resource that students can draw on.

Indeed, the evidence suggests that effective teachers talk more than ineffective ones, not less. Barak Rosenshine's work on effective instruction noted that effective maths teachers were, on average, spending twenty-three minutes over the course of a forty-minute lesson talking to their students, compared to less effective teachers who spent only eleven minutes doing so.[3] Clearly, avoiding explanation isn't the answer to better teaching, but this doesn't mean that all explanation is equal. We can see in the case of Sarah at the start of the chapter that an explanation can be very interesting and detailed, but this doesn't mean it will be memorable.

Explaining something well takes thought, care and planning. The rest of this chapter considers strategies for

---

3 Barak Rosenshine, Principles of Instruction: Research-Based Strategies That All Teachers Should Know, *American Educator* 36(1) (2012): 12–19, 39 at 14. Available at: https://www.aft.org/sites/default/files/periodicals/Rosenshine.pdf.

making explanation as effective as possible in supporting learning.

1. Plan Carefully

What do you need to say?

Looking back to when I started teaching, I think I was over-confident in my ability to explain geographical concepts successfully. When planning lessons, I would simply think "and here is where I'll explain the atmospheric circulation model" and move on. Big mistake! It wouldn't be until I had actually started to try to explain something that I'd realise either that my subject knowledge wasn't as good as I had thought it was or, more commonly, that I wasn't quite sure how to explain it. Explanation needs a lot more planning and thought than this.

In his book *Mining for Gold*, Fergal Roche reflects on the excellent teachers he has come across during his own education and career.[4] One thing that he remarks on is the habit that some of these teachers had of coming into class with notes to use in their lesson; not something that I have seen in fourteen years of teaching, but something that I now do regularly myself.

Having learnt my lesson, when teaching a topic for the first time I now try to think much more carefully about what it is that I want students to know or be able to do by the end of my explanation and then work backwards from that. I start by considering the knowledge they already have and whether there is anything further they need to know to access what I am about to say. For example, if I want to discuss the management of endangered wetland ecosystems, I will start by explaining what we mean by endangered, show images of wetlands and remind them of the definition of an ecosystem. Returning to previous knowledge is vitally important when building an explanation. Rosenshine's research also suggests that the most effective teachers spend a significant proportion of the lesson on recap.[5]

When planning our explanations we need to consider the following questions:

- What else do the students need to know if they are going to understand this? For example, the definition of key words, background information on the place being used as an example, details about the location and so on.

- How can this explanation help them to picture what is being said? For example, would the use of images, diagrams and maps aid understanding?

- What will they struggle with the most and how will we support them with this? For example, by using repetition, notes and visual prompts.

- What *must* they remember at the end of this explanation? For example, identify the threshold concepts or key pieces

4 Fergal Roche, *Mining for Gold: Stories of Effective Teachers* (Woodbridge: John Catt Educational, 2017).

5 Rosenshine, Principles of Instruction, 13.

of information that we would expect them to be able to recall in a few weeks' time.

♦ How can this be explained in a way that will support their working memory? For example, through the use of dual coding, analogies, examples and stories.

The other strategies in this chapter look at this process, and the research behind it, in more detail.

2. Know What They Know

What errors are they likely to make?

The more we know about our audience the better we can tailor our explanation. This is one reason why it is easier to teach a class with which you are familiar than one which is new. Research by David Berliner and colleagues showed that teachers who were highly effective in their usual school and setting became unhappy and less effective when put in front of a different class.[6]

If I am going to teach a lesson on the impact of deforestation in Brazil, it helps if I know whether my students know anything about Brazil's level of development and patterns of settlement, about the idea of net primary productivity and about the factors influencing rates of surface run-off. I can teach them about deforestation without this previous knowledge, but I will need to explain it differently. A well-planned curriculum is at the heart of all that we do, including explanation.

It is important to make sure that students have actually learnt what you intended them to. This is difficult as

6   David C. Berliner et al., Implications of Research on Pedagogical Expertise and Experience for Mathematics Teaching. In Douglas A. Grouws and Thomas J. Cooney (eds), *Perspectives on Research on Effective Mathematics Teaching* (Reston, VI: National Council of Teachers of Mathematics, 1988), pp. 67–95.

learning is invisible and, consequently, we can find ourselves reaching for what Robert Coe terms "poor proxies for learning".[7] These are surface indicators rather than deep measures of learning – for example, students seeming engaged or producing high-quality work in their books. Instead, we need to check what they have learnt using quick low-stakes quizzes, so we can see what they have actually remembered and can recall on demand.

We can also try to adapt our explanations to take into account misconceptions that students are likely to have and to address them before they become embedded. A lot of this awareness comes with the experience of having explained the same concept several times and dealt with recurring misconceptions. It is worth considering likely misconceptions as a department when planning new schemes of work. I now find it impossible to teach anything about a given African country without first reiterating that Africa is a diverse continent and that we should avoid talking about it as though it were a homogenous entity, or to teach about climate change without reminding students that it has nothing to do with holes in the ozone layer. Other common examples to look out for include:

- The soil in the rainforest is very fertile.

- Rising sea levels are caused by the melting of sea ice.

- Rivers start at the sea.

- Migration is driven by the climate or by tourist attractions.

- People in low-income countries (LICs) are able to just move and build homes closer to the water supply.

- Printing more money will make countries wealthier.

---

7   Robert Coe, *Improving Education: A Triumph of Hope over Experience*, Inaugural Lecture of Professor Robert Coe, Durham University, 18 June 2013. Available at: http://www.cem.org/attachments/publications/ImprovingEducation2013.pdf, p. 12.

A lot of this misinformation can be drawn out and addressed through questioning (see Chapter 6).

3. Use Analogies

How can we link new knowledge to something familiar?

Students are more likely to remember your explanation of a new concept if they can relate it to something well-known. This is where analogies come in. It can be hard to understand an explanation of low pressure on the equator using unfamiliar geographical terms, but far easier if you start by thinking about how a hot air balloon rises up. Students may struggle with your explanation of the role of groundwater stores when thinking about water surplus and deficit, but an analogy of a bank account, with money coming in and out, can help them to picture what you mean and to make sense of it conceptually.

As you teach certain topics, over time, you will build up your bank of analogies. However, if you are teaching something new, or teaching something that you know students typically struggle with, it is worth spending some time planning the analogies that you will use.

The aim of the analogy is to make the abstract – for example, warm air rising on the equator to create low pressure – more concrete – such as using the visual image of the hot air balloon. We want our students to be able to picture what that abstract idea might look like if made physical, and so analogies are best drawn from things they have seen or experienced themselves. Fellow teachers have offered the following examples of how they use a visual image to illustrate a concept:

♦ A duvet trapping in body heat at night – cloud cover or greenhouse gases.

♦ A bottle of water you put in the freezer then gets distorted as the ice expands – freeze-thaw weathering.

♦ The end of the toothpaste tube getting blocked – the vent of a volcano.

♦ Layering make-up on your face – contour lines.

♦ Interlocking your fingers – picturing how interlocking spurs appear in a river valley.

♦ Walking around the classroom and weaving past obstructions – river meanders.

♦ Pushing through any obstructions in the classroom in a straight line – glacial valleys.

4. Tell Stories

How can we harness the power of stories?

Watching great geography teachers at work often reminds me of great storytellers. Their explanation has a clear rhythm to it; there is a beginning, a middle and a sense of building towards a conclusion. Whether they are aware of it or not, they are tapping into a powerful way of making their explanation memorable: the power of stories. As with analogies, the use of stories helps to make the abstract more concrete and helps make your explanation stick.

In *Why Don't Students Like School?*, Daniel Willingham explains that humans seem predisposed to remember information when framed as stories and explores how we can exploit this fact in our teaching. He refers to the four Cs of stories as causality, conflict, complication and character, and suggests that we build these into our explanation of the concepts we want students to remember.[8] This is especially useful in geography as the case studies and examples we use to root our theory in the real world can easily be structured as a story. You could teach the formation of a tropical storm as a list of factors you want students to remember or you could invoke the power of story:

> *"It was the end of a long, hot summer and the ocean was warm. The moist air rose quickly in the tropics and the wind picked up, swirling around this point of low pressure. Katrina was born."*

Having established the causality, you could then pick out a character from Hurricane Katrina, such as a person living in the French Quarter of New Orleans, and tell the story of the hurricane from their perspective. The conflict is between the city and the weather – personified as a character itself – with the complications being the attempts to keep the population safe and distribute aid following the disaster.

If I am teaching the potential pitfalls of aid projects and the problems with misguided development efforts, I reach for news stories of tractors left rusting in north Africa where the local conditions weren't considered when planning for a

---

8   Willingham, *Why Don't Students Like School?*, pp. 67–71.

"green revolution"[9] and of women left turning abandoned Playpumps in South Africa after the children decided that roundabouts were only a fun game for a while.[10] Of course, I can only reach for these stories because I know them myself. This is yet another reminder that our subject knowledge is of critical importance.

5. Case Studies and Examples

How do we choose the examples to illustrate what we say?

One of the things that makes geography such a rewarding subject to teach is the choice we have over the case studies and examples we use to demonstrate the theory or model we

9   See Kurt Gerhardt, Why Development Aid for Africa Has Failed, *Spiegel Online* (16 August 2010). Available at: http://www.spiegel.de/international/world/time-for-a-rethink-why-development-aid-for-africa-has-failed-a-712068.html.

10 See Andrew Chambers, Africa's Not-So-Magic Roundabout, *The Guardian* (24 November 2009). Available at: https://www.theguardian.com/commentisfree/2009/nov/24/africa-charity-water-pumps-roundabouts.

are studying. It is one area of the national curriculum, and of the exam specifications, in which teachers actually have a huge amount of freedom. The selection of the best possible case study or example can make an explanation all the more powerful and memorable.

This is another area of lesson design in which a teacher's expert subject knowledge comes into play. It is very difficult to think of an example of a multilateral aid scheme or an area of the world with effective river management if you don't have this knowledge to hand. We also risk using the same places to typify the same content every time and this can lead to students having a very shallow understanding of certain places. Bangladesh becomes little more than land threatened by rising sea levels and Brazil no more than its favelas.

One way to avoid this is to ensure that there are a few examples that you keep referring back to throughout a key stage, or even plan to revisit across different key stages. For instance, you might look at Lagos to demonstrate the pressures of urban growth, return to Nigeria when looking at the transition from LIC to newly emerging economy (NEE) and then again to explore sustainable development. There is always a tension between wanting students to have an in-depth understanding of given examples or a broad knowledge of different places around the world, but if we focus on the latter we risk creating poor geographers. By returning to the same location in different contexts, we also allow for retrieval practice to strengthen recall (for more on this see Chapter 6).

The world is rapidly changing, and it is important that our use of examples changes with it. In the last year, I have come across geography lessons that still use the tiger economies of south-east Asia as examples of NEEs, when those in Africa might be more revealing. I have also seen the example of Brazil used as a place where deforestation rates are increasing, even though they have been falling there for some time and Indonesia might actually be a better example of a place where they are rising. We need to re-evaluate our schemes of work regularly and update them to reflect our changing planet.

6. Support Working Memory

How do we make the explanation stick?

One problem with explanation, and perhaps a reason for the persistence of the myths of the cone of learning – that students won't remember what they are told, is that spoken words are transient. There is nothing to refer back to. If we give students too much new information we run the risk of overloading their memory and much of what we say will be forgotten. We need to find ways of supporting their working memory to make sure that they can recall what we have said and apply it to their work.

One important way to support students' working memory is to limit distractions. This could include distractions in the environment – such as visual clutter at the front of the room that draws focus – distractions from each other – such as irrelevant questions or disruptive behaviour – or distractions within the explanation – such as interesting tangents and supplementary information.[11] To avoid these distractions, we need to make sure that our classrooms are as free from visual noise as possible. This can be difficult if the school policy calls for the display of behaviour policies, reward systems, literacy policies, key word lists and so on. If you must display these, keep them neat and as unobtrusive as your school will allow.

In some subjects it might be useful to have visual prompts on display – for example, commonly misspelt words, key equations and so on. The problem is that geography is such a vast subject, you would need to change these displays every time a topic changed – and do so for up to seven different year groups all studying very different things. Any generic display left up will be of limited use. Better to add the salient and topic-specific information to your whiteboard as and when you need it.

We can also aim to avoid interruptions by making sure that students understand when it is appropriate to ask a question and how to do so. Few things derail a carefully planned explanation as quickly as a hand going up and a little voice saying, "It's not to do with this topic but ..." The same goes for requesting to borrow a pen during an explanation, or anything else that draws attention from what is being said. It is worth establishing the ground rules early on and making their purpose clear.

Distractions from within an explanation can be the most difficult to target. Geography is a fascinating subject and there are always links to almost-relevant little diversions; however, exploring these can make it more difficult for students to follow and remember the main information you

---

11 For more on the impact of cluttered classrooms see Jamie Thom, *Slow Teaching: On Finding Calm, Clarity and Impact in the Classroom* (Woodbridge: John Catt Educational, 2018).

want them to learn (for more on dealing with this see Chapter 6). This is one reason why it helps to plan out your explanation in advance. Consider carefully whether your asides are adding interest or whether they have the potential to distract.

Another way to support students in following your explanation is to make notes of the key points on the board as you are speaking so there is a record that they can refer back to afterwards. These prompts could also take the form of diagrams or mind maps, designed to make your schema – your own mental map of the topic – visible to the students. Avoid making this too complicated and instead focus on the key information you want them to include when they are working on their task later. A visualiser can be a useful way of making sure you can add and display notes without constantly turning your back to the class and breaking the flow of your explanation.

You can also take advantage of the principles of dual coding. This is the theory that we are able to take in information using both visual and auditory processes and by using both it makes the information more memorable and easier to recollect.[12] This is where geography teachers can really play to their strengths as we are used to drawing on visual elements to aid our explanations. It would be very unusual to find a geography teacher who would explain the formation of stacks without leaping to the board to draw the process or explain the growth of cities following the pattern shown in the Burgess model without using a diagram of it. Unlike the generic displays discussed earlier, these are clearly linked to the topic at hand and show only information that is currently relevant; those things you want a student to be thinking about here and now.

---

12 Richard E. Mayer and Richard B. Anderson, Animations Need Narrations: An Experimental Test of a Dual-Coding Hypothesis, *Journal of Educational Psychology* 83(4) (1991): 484–490.

Case Study: Explanation

Ed Leighton, director of research and learning, St Joseph's College

For me, the first rule of explanation is that "passion is contagious". I can still remember my old geography teacher telling stories about his trips to Canada and Italy. His passion for the subject really shone through and that's where my love of geography started. Your explanations are nothing without passion. It needs to come across that the main reason behind your explanation is to transmit amazing geographical knowledge that will help students to understand and transform the world, not just pass an exam.

One of my colleagues is an absolute expert at explanations. When talking to my A level students about her, they said, "It's like an A* answer is coming out of her mouth." She models the language and repeats key words over and over again until it sticks with them. It's clear that she really knows her stuff! When getting students to explain key concepts back to her, she is relentless in getting them to use the correct language. Students repeat their explanations until they achieve a better standard.

Telling stories is a key part of geographical explanations. We try to find the real-life stories of the people behind the case study knowledge. When telling stories we use metaphors, analogies, rich imagery and vivid language. There is always a story to tell in geography, but sometimes we need to look hard for it. *National Geographic* is a great place to start.[13] A powerful story helps to bring geography to life.

An authentic explanation takes practice. At first I really struggled with my explanation of magma plumes and their relationship to plate tectonics, so I rehearsed the explanation many times. When I filmed myself and played it back, I

---

13 See https://nationalgeographic.com/.

noticed that I was talking far too fast. I slowed down my explanations and introduced more pauses, as I realised I was cognitively overloading students. From my stuttering and rambling it was obvious that I didn't know my subject well enough, so I went away and read up on magma plumes and how they form. I used the whiteboard to draw diagrams to back up my explanation. This dual-coding approach allowed students to see a visual interpretation of my words. Once I had finished my explanation, I then got students to summarise what I had explained in their own words. This means that students have to think hard during my teacher-led explanation, as I will be checking for understanding.

PowerPoint slides or knowledge organisers are very important but have no emotional impact, so I deliver explanations using multisensory experiences. I use powerful photos, video clips and diagrams and try to take the students outside the classroom as often as possible. In the classroom, I try to use props as often as I can to explain concepts in a novel way: to make the abstract concrete. Whether that's pushing tables apart to show a constructive plate boundary, mixing sand with water to show suspension or throwing balls of paper against the wall to represent abrasion.

In summary, high-quality teacher-led explanations are vital in geography. The craft of developing a perfect explanation takes time and practice. It requires high levels of subject knowledge but also needs to be delivered in an engaging way that makes students think and remember.

Chapter 3
Modelling

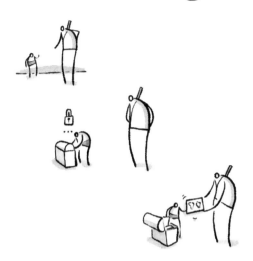

Emma

Emma is in Year 7 and is completing her first piece of extended project work: a comparison between Uganda and the UK. She has started by drawing an outline of the two countries and their flags. She wants to compare their climates and knows what the average temperature is in Uganda but isn't sure what it is in the UK so makes up a figure that sounds about right. She writes several pages about Uganda and then several pages about the UK. She is really pleased with her work. She will be disappointed with the feedback.

Rasul

In the classroom next door, Rasul is completing the same task. He is finding the process much easier. The teacher has carefully explained the major differences between Uganda and the UK and has given the class a handout containing all the information they need. He has, thoughtfully, provided a model answer to the task, which Rasul is painstakingly copying out. After all, if this is a model answer, it isn't likely that he will be able to improve upon it.

Modelling is a tricky business. Too little can leave students unsure of the expectations you have for their work and blind to what a finished piece should look like. Think how hard it would be to complete a jigsaw puzzle without the picture on the lid of the box. However, model too much, or in the wrong way, and their practice can be devoid of the "thinking hard" that makes the learning stick (see Chapter 4 for more on this).

Modelling in the classroom could be defined simply as "showing students what their finished work should look like". In practice, however, it is much more complex. We don't just want to show students a finished article; we want to develop their metacognition, the ways in which they think about their learning, so that they understand why their work should look like this.[1] They need to be able to apply what they have learnt during the modelling process in different situations for it to be of any use. We can see how, while Rasul may be able to write a good comparative piece about Uganda and the UK – albeit only through mimicry – he is unlikely to have developed any understanding about what makes a good piece of writing. He won't be able to apply this model to a piece of work comparing two other countries or to a different comparative task.

This is why modelling is so tied up with the art of explanation. We need to demonstrate how to build up to the finished piece of work in a clear and methodical way that also allows our students to understand our thought processes. It is important that we don't miss out steps or assume a level of prior knowledge. What might seem obvious and

---

1   For more on this see Chapter 13 in Alex Quigley's *The Confident Teacher: Developing Successful Habits of Mind, Body and Pedagogy* (Abingdon: Routledge, 2016).

straightforward to us – such as labelling the axes of a graph, starting with the background in a field sketch or not making up facts for the sake of convenience – will be less obvious to them.

A lack of effective modelling can lead to students becoming quickly demotivated as they work hard to produce what they think we are asking for, only to be told afterwards that their efforts are flawed. For students to believe that they can be successful in geography, they first need the support that will allow them to experience the feeling of success. By modelling and carefully scaffolding answers, we can show them what we are looking for and how to achieve it, allowing them to see what is possible.

I would suggest that modelling is even more important in geography than in many other subjects. Many students arrive at secondary school having had very little specialist input in our subject and many have only a tentative grasp of what geography really entails. Like many teachers, I start my first lesson with a new Year 7 class with the question, "What is geography and what geography have you done before?" The answers tend to be limited to countries, maps and maybe rivers. Students haven't developed a broader understanding of the subject in the way they may have in history, English or maths.

The first step to modelling geographical work is to be clear on what geography actually involves. Students need to see examples of excellent geographical work alongside the topics they will study. This is where corridor displays can play a role, as long as students are directed to really look at them. There can be a tendency to display work showing either extended writing or poster work – selected for its presentation – but try to include a full range of geographical work. This could include a thorough interpretation of data shown in a graph, the use of map evidence to draw a conclusion, or diagrams of key physical processes. In all cases, it is important to clearly annotate the work to show why you consider it to be excellent so that the audience understands how to apply the message to their own work.

Also consider keeping a portfolio of excellent work over the year, whether on paper or digitally, to show students.[2] This gives you the opportunity to really unpick the work with your class and to ensure that they fully understand why it is being held up as good. They can also use this archive of excellence to contrast with their own work before redrafting and making improvements. Our goal is to give them a feel for where they are going, to show them the lid of the jigsaw box, so that they have an awareness of the bigger picture of the subject.

You could design a display to show the nature of the subject by focusing on the links between the different topics that students will study with you. Place a map of their community in the centre with annotation around it showing, for example, how the area links to different trade routes, the physical processes occurring along nearby rivers, images of the surrounding landscape, diagrams of how it formed and an exploration of the environmental impact of the settlement. Even just drawing on our little corner of East Sussex, at my school we could consider the tectonic forces that lifted our landscape into the Weald anticline, how the straightening of the Cuckmere River made trade easier and how the rise of Transition Town projects have addressed environmental concerns. This kind of display would help to model how a geographer sees a location.

This kind of exposure to the true nature of the subject is only the first step, however. The rest of this chapter considers the strategies we can use to build up models with students so that they really understand what we mean when we talk about excellent geography.

---

2   For a detailed discussion on the use of portfolios of student work see: Ron Berger, *An Ethic of Excellence: Building a Culture of Craftsmanship with Students* (Portsmouth, NH: Heinemann, 2003).

1. Choosing to Model

What do we need to model?

When I first started teaching, I didn't model anywhere near enough. This was in part because when I trained we were encouraged – or in many cases instructed – to strictly limit the time we spent at the front of the class. Fundamentally, however, I didn't fully understand the importance of modelling. I hoped that students would work it out for themselves. This meant I would set them a task, such as drawing a climate graph, with only the most minimal of instruction and then spend the rest of the lesson running from student to student in order to guide them all in what they needed to do. From practical experience, this clearly isn't the best approach. Additionally, there has since been clear research that outlines how limiting instruction in this way is counterproductive.[3]

I am now much more methodical in how I approach modelling. The first time students are exposed to a new skill or approach, I model it very thoroughly – sometimes with them working with me step by step. If I am teaching them how to draw a climate graph, we will draw it together as I explain why I am taking each step – for example, adding the intervals on the axis, showing the temperature on a line graph but precipitation using a bar graph and so on. Once we have a model to follow, they can then complete their own using a set of similar data. The next step is to give them a task which uses the same skill but adapts the method slightly – such as producing a climate graph with temperatures below freezing.

The next time they encounter the same skill I will just run through the basics once more and focus on common errors – such as confusing the line and bar graphs. I let them practise while I circulate and monitor. At subsequent revisits, I

---

3   Kirschner, Sweller and Clark, Why Minimal Guidance during Instruction Does Not Work.

expect most of the class to remember how to do it themselves and can focus on supporting those students who have previously struggled.

This approach to modelling works for all sorts of geographical skills – for example, cartographic skills, collecting and displaying data, carrying out a cost-benefit analysis and writing a comparison between two places. We need to remember that students will encounter many things in our classrooms that are second nature to us but that they are being exposed to for the first time. This curse of knowledge – the problem we have when the more we know about something, the harder it is to see things from the perspective of those without that knowledge – can mean that our initial expectations of what students can do without support are too high.[4] We don't want to lower the bar of our expectations, so instead we need to model exactly how to reach it.

2. Using Exemplars

How do we expose students to great work?

An exemplar is a piece of work that demonstrates the standard you are expecting. It is important to note that by this, we mean the expected standard for a student at that stage of their education. If we take the example at the start of this chapter, a piece of excellent writing contrasting Uganda and the UK would look very different at A level than it would in Year 7. This is one reason why it helps to have a very clear idea in your own mind of what an excellent piece of work looks like at each different stage (see Chapter 1).

---

4   For a detailed look at the phenomenon of the curse of knowledge, see: David Didau, Are Teachers Cursed with Knowledge?, *The Learning Spy* [blog] (5 September 2016). Available at: http://www.learningspy.co.uk/featured/teachers-cursed-knowledge/.

Simply showing students exemplar answers is unlikely to make much of an impact, especially if they simply believe that this standard is beyond them. Instead, we need to break exemplars down into their component parts so that students can see how they work and why they are of a high standard. For this reason, it is a good idea to annotate any exemplar work you display to make how it has met the success criteria very clear.

A potential pitfall of using exemplars is that students may simply copy the example without really developing any understanding. A simple solution to this problem is to use exemplars that focus on geographical skill rather than specific task completion. For example, show them an exemplar answer to a question about the distribution of cities in the UK before asking them a question about the distribution of temperate forests. That way you can highlight the common features of a descriptive answer – such as the need to explain the general pattern, give specific examples and identify anomalies – without giving away the answer to the question. We want students to have to think hard about their answer rather than mimicking examples.

Therefore, when giving an exemplar answer, you need to spend time working through it as a class and looking at what makes it a good piece of work. Give them things to look for, such as the use of specific facts and figures or the use of key geographical terms from the topic. Also look at the way the answer has been structured. Help them to identify a logical structure and discuss how this comes from planning an answer before you begin writing. Look at the way it builds towards a conclusion. These are all things that students often struggle with, especially in Key Stage 3, where they may be used to focusing on writing about a topic rather than answering an extended question.

The following example is a piece I use with students at the beginning of Year 7 before asking them to write a piece of extended writing comparing Uganda and the UK. As you can see, the exemplar compares the UK and India, to avoid the issue of students copying the example. I ask students to pick apart the exemplar piece to explore why it is of a high standard. First, we explore the different structural features of the report, and I ask them to:

♦ Highlight each explanation of a point.

♦ Underline any direct comparisons made between the UK and India.

♦ Circle any specific facts which are used to support a point.

Then we explore more open questions about the piece:

♦ What does the introduction do?

♦ What is the conclusion for?

♦ What makes this an example of an excellent piece of work?

How does India compare to the UK?

Introduction

When comparing countries, you can consider both the physical geography (the things that are naturally occurring and not created by people) and the human geography (the differences that people have created). This report will compare the UK and India in terms of climate, landscape, level of wealth and the health of the people. In its conclusion, this report will show that these differences are all connected to each other.

Climate

The UK is located in the North Atlantic Ocean and its climate is mild with rain throughout the year. The average winter temperature is 7°C and the summer average is 18°C. This means that farming can only happen during the spring and summer as there is not enough sunlight for plants to grow in the winter. In contrast, much of India is hot all year round with the temperature rarely dropping below 20°C. It has a wet season and a dry season and farming has to take this into account. It does mean that they can grow more food on a piece of land as they can often have more than one harvest during the year.

Landscape

The UK is roughly split into two halves – with low mountains and hills found in the north and west, and low land found more in the south and east. The south and east are naturally dominated by oak woodland, whereas the north typically has pine forests and moorland. India is a much larger country and has a much greater range of landscapes. The north is dominated by the Himalayan mountains, which are the highest on Earth. The great Thar desert is in the north-west as the monsoon rains do not reach this far in the wet season. The south is closer to the equator and is more tropical. The centre of India is dominated by great plains and river systems that provide water to the farmers. The size of the country and large natural features in the landscape, such as mountains and deserts, can make transport and communication difficult.

Levels of wealth

One of the biggest differences between the UK and India is in how rich the two countries are. The UK has a GDP per capita of US$41,000 whereas India's is only US$1,500. This is because many people in India are farmers who don't receive very much money for their crops, whereas people in the UK are often employed in higher paying service jobs. Because the UK is wealthier, the government can afford to provide free schooling and so literacy rates in the UK are at almost 100%, whereas in India they are still only at 74%, although this has been improving rapidly.

There are some material signs of wealth in India as people increasingly use smartphones and companies like Microsoft have been opening there to take advantage of the improvement in education.

Health

Another big difference between the UK and India is that people in the UK on average live to the age of 81, whereas in India the average life expectancy is only 66. This is because the UK can provide free healthcare to all its population and people generally live relatively close to health centres. Some people in India live a very long way from the nearest doctor and can't afford to pay for medicine.

Conclusion

I feel that the most significant difference between the UK and India is that the UK has a higher level of economic development and can therefore afford better education and healthcare. This means that people in the UK usually have a better quality of life. This difference could also be due to physical factors, as the landscape in the UK could make it easier to transport goods and so make money, while in terms of health the tropical climate in India makes diseases like malaria more likely.

There are similarities between the countries as both are becoming more wealthy, and the new companies moving to India could mean that eventually the human geography of India becomes very similar to that in the UK.

3. Going Live

When should we create the model?

Models can be created in advance, but we can also produce them live, working through the steps with the class in real time, as in the example of producing a climate graph. The advantage of this kind of live modelling is that it allows you to explain your thought processes as you tackle the task.

The sticking point for many students when they try to start a piece of extended writing is in writing an effective first line. Live modelling gives you the opportunity to show how to keep this simple and launch straight into the answer. For example, take the question, "Assess the extent to which the primary effects of tectonic hazards are more significant than the secondary effects."

I would begin to live model my answer by writing:

"It could be argued that secondary effects, those created as a result of the primary effects, are actually more significant than the initial primary effects because …"

As I am writing this opening, I can explain that I am starting by saying "It could be argued" because I want to make it clear that I am going to be making a judgement after considering both sides. I am adding a definition of secondary effects to show the reader that I know the difference between primary and secondary. I am including the words "more significant than" to link my answer clearly to the question.

Live modelling allows us to show how we make corrections and edits to our work and that we do this as an ongoing process. It also means that we can discuss what makes a good geographical answer and how this might be distinct from an answer in other subjects. Good geographical writing tends to be more precise and to the point than what students are encouraged to produce in English classes, for example. If they are just being tested on their ability to use facts to make a point, not on their ability to remember *accurate* facts, students are sometimes encouraged to make up details to include in non-fiction writing in English exams, but this is not an approach that they should employ in geography. We can emphasise these differences when we model live.

Another approach to live modelling is to build up the answer with the class through questioning. Once you have the opening line you can then turn to the students, prompting them to see what they would add next. In the example on page 57 you might ask one student for an example of a serious secondary effect of tectonic hazards and then another for a case study example to illustrate its impact, all the while explaining why you need to include these components.[5]

4. Search and Destroy

Do we only model excellent work?

One problem with only showing excellent work is that it can fail to address students' common misconceptions and mistakes. For this reason, it is often useful to provide models at a range of standards and to unpick the features that makes one more successful than another.

This strategy can be used in any lesson but is especially effective after a mock exam. If many students in the class struggled with a particular question, produce an answer that contains an amalgamation of the errors they made. Ask them to pick through the piece and identify the mistakes.

---

5   For an example of how these answers can be built up by questioning, see: Mark Enser, Model Live, *Heathfield Teach Share Blog* [blog] (9 January 2017). Available at: https://heathfieldteachshare.wordpress.com/2017/01/09/model-live/.

Here's an example of an answer to the question, "To what extent can urban planning strategies in an LIC or NEE help the urban poor? Use an example of an urban area you have studied."

Modelling errors

Eko Atlantic is a development in Lagos, Nigeria, that is being created on the coast from land reclaimed from the sea. This development is designed to be the new financial and commercial hub of the city and will also contain many luxury apartments. They are also including a new water treatment works for the community and better transport links through the integrated LAMATA scheme. This project will help the city because it is providing jobs, water and better transport. It is also making new land, which is good because Lagos is running out of space.

They should be able to see that the example chosen is of limited use as it wasn't designed to help the urban poor, the answer hasn't considered the original conditions that needed to be improved, there is little discussion of the "extent" to which strategies have worked and there isn't a conclusion. These are all common errors that students make when answering this type of question and have been specifically chosen here to model these mistakes.

Our goal is to develop self-regulation in students. We want to them to reach the stage where they know what a good answer looks like – and what a bad one looks like – and have the ability to evaluate and adapt their own work as they are producing it. To this end, we can produce exemplars that don't just typify the very best or worst answers but a range in between. Ask students to come up with the criteria for an excellent answer to a particular question and then use this to evaluate and rank a range of example answers, justifying their decisions. Following this, they can go on to write their own answer to a similar question, using the same success criteria. This should give them an excellent understanding of the standard required and, importantly, the experience of applying this understanding to a range of questions.

5. Talk the Walk

How do we model "thinking like a geographer"?

It could be argued that we study geography in order to see the world differently. In the preface to *Teaching Geography 11–18*, the authors discuss a photograph of Royston Heath; looking at it as geographers to unpick what the landscape can reveal.[6] They draw on inferences from the photograph itself as well as on their wider knowledge of the area and on the theories underpinning human and physical geography to give what they call a "'geographical' account" of the place.[7] This is what we mean by "thinking like a geographer".

Many of our students are unlikely to experience people looking at the world in this way outside of the classroom, and can look only to us to model this approach. We can

---

6 David Lambert and John Morgan, *Teaching Geography 11–18: A Conceptual Approach* (Maidenhead: Open University Press, 2010).

7 Lambert and Morgan, *Teaching Geography 11–18*, ix.

achieve this by modelling this way of looking at the world in our explanations.

When explaining the role of the British Empire in shaping contemporary Nigeria, we can begin by making our use of historical fact explicit. Then we can show how a geographer will combine this with their knowledge of the physical geography of the region to explain how the colony helped to give the empire a comparative advantage, thereby also drawing on a concept from economics. This compartmentalised approach to geography gives many opportunities to model thinking geographically. It allows you to demonstrate how the various themes students have studied come together to create a better understanding of a place. Other examples of drawing on multiple themes to this end could include:

◆ Haiti – tectonics, tropical storms, development, trade and colonialism.

◆ London – location of settlement, flood defences, geology, water supply, ecological footprint, changing demographics and migration.

◆ India – employment structures, the impact of transnational corporations (TNCs), low-pressure weather systems, tectonics and the landscape.

This ability to draw on a wide range of disciplines to provide a geographical account is central to our discipline but is not something our students will recognise unless we explicitly model it, and highlight when we do so, as we talk.[8]

---

8   Standish, The Place of Regional Geography.

6. Removing the Scaffolding

When do we stop modelling?

There comes a time when we need to stop providing so many models, remove this layer of scaffolding, and leave the students to stand on their own two feet. If we don't, they can become very reliant on the support offered by model answers, or supportive structures like sentence starters, and can struggle to practise without them.

If your students have become over-reliant on support, you might want to look again at how you are using modelling. As discussed, ideally you want to model how to carry out the type of task, and the processes and skills students will need, rather than giving away the answers to the practice questions. Over time, students should be able to refer back to their previous experiences of working with the aid of a model and apply this when they encounter something similar again.

Using, and removing, scaffolding takes careful planning and a long view through the curriculum. If you know that students are going to encounter and practise decision-making six times throughout the year, for example, you might plan the first time to be very heavily modelled with the use of exemplars. The second time you could plan to live model one paragraph before leaving them to complete the rest, with further support available for those who need it. The next time they could begin by reviewing what they have written, using the "search and destroy" strategy to spot and correct their own errors before you give them a few prompts to help them structure their answer.

For example, you might give students a task to decide whether a reservoir should be built for their local community. They are going to use a range of geographical maps and data to help them reach a decision. As this is the first time they are going to carry out this type of task, you could give them a full exemplar of this kind of writing and show them how sources should be used to make and develop points and reach a conclusion.

The second time they tackle a decision-making task, you might ask them to decide which aid project would be the most suitable for a region in East Africa. You could ask them to first review their last decision-making activity to see what made this a good piece of work, before modelling the first paragraph of this new task. They can use the model paragraph to continue their answer and reach a conclusion. While they are doing this you might need to give some sentence starters to those students who are struggling to get going.

The next decision-making task could be on the topic of drilling for oil in the Arctic. Remind them of the criteria of a good decision-making answer – for example, uses data, is specifically relevant to the area, includes the views of stake holders, considers sustainability and so on. Obviously this criteria will vary depending on the key stage. Ask them to review their previous piece of work with this criteria in mind and pick out any errors they need to learn from in this next task.

In each case the topic they are writing about is very different, and they will need to learn a lot of specific information about each issue, but, more than this, you are drawing out the common subject-specific skills they need through careful modelling and scaffolding. By the time they get to the end of the year they should be able to carry out a decision-making task for themselves without the use of further models.

Many geography departments have developed their own way of providing models for their classes. The example that follows is from head of geography Michael Chiles.

Case Study: Modelling

Michael Chiles, head of geography, Ormiston Bolingbroke Academy

In our department, we have used CPD time to ensure that all teachers have a clear understanding of what excellence looks like in geography. This was a key component to establish before we could embed modelling into our everyday teaching practice. This has led to a writing structure known as PDL (point, develop, link), which allows all students to apply their understanding to exam-style questions in order to maximise their marks:

♦ Make a **point** – for example: "One way in which global inequality can be reduced is through remittances."

♦ **Develop** the point – for example: "This is when migrants send money back to family members living in their country of origin."

♦ **Link** your point back to the question – for example: "This reduces global inequality because the family members can use this money to pay for key living essentials."

Alongside knowing what excellence looks like, teachers need to establish a conducive learning environment in the classroom, thereby ensuring that strategies such as live modelling can be used. Ben Newmark has outlined the foundations needed to set up a learning environment that allows modelling strategies to flourish.[9] One of the strategies Newmark talks about is the need for teachers to teach students to listen; you need all thirty pairs of eyes focused on your every move as you demonstrate excellence.

As I write this, it is now my second academic year as head of department and we have trained students to "actively listen"

---

9   Ben Newmark, Ten principles for Great Explicit Teaching, *BENNEWMARK* [blog] (7 October 2017). Available at: https://bennewmark.wordpress.com/2017/10/07/ten-principles-for-great-explict-teaching/.

by having nothing in their hands when we are talking. Initially, this took time to embed and required endless persistence and patience. However, I can now see the benefits, as fewer students ask, "Sir, what do we need to do?" at the end of demonstrations. In a recent lesson with Year 7, the department used visualisers to demonstrate how to draw river cross-section profiles – an inherently difficult skill for GCSE students. Through the insistence on active listening during the demonstration, students set about plotting their own profiles with greater success.

Effective modelling, as outlined by Shaun Allison and Andy Tharby in *Making Every Lesson Count*, requires the use of strong questioning, timely feedback and an understanding of what excellence looks like to enable students to develop independence.

We have developed the following modelling strategies to guide students towards that independence:

♦ Live modelling using the classroom whiteboard – with students coming up to the board to indicate where the PDL sentences are within the answer, as well as finishing off answers by adding the link aspect to completed point and develop sentences.

♦ Using completed answers – *Blue Peter* style – with students highlighting where the PDL sentences are and then using this model as support when writing their own answer.

♦ Using poor examples so students can spot the mistakes and make the necessary improvements to make it the "perfect answer".

♦ Displaying a gallery of excellence in each classroom to show what excellence looks like for each different style of exam question.

♦ Capturing excellence during the lesson by spotting examples of students' work and displaying them on the visualiser to showcase to the rest of the class.

Chapter 4

Practice

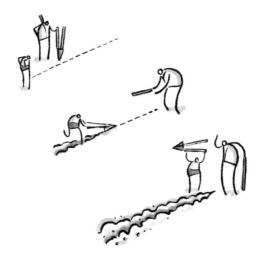

Mr Jones

Mr Jones stands in front of his Year 7 class with a growing sense of frustration. "Let's try again. Who can tell me what we mean by erosion?" The class look at him blankly. "Remember? We did it at the start of the year. I mentioned it at the end of the last lesson." Still nothing. "We watched a clip about it. I drew a diagram. You copied down the definition." Nothing.

Mr Jones is baffled. He knows they did this, so why don't they remember it?

Shaun

Shaun is drawing yet another climate graph. The class have practised this a lot and he can do it on automatic now. In fact, it is so easy he isn't sure why they are bothering to do it again. He finishes and looks at his work. There is the line graph to show precipitation and the bar graph showing temperature. Just like the last time he practised. Easy.

Practice sits at the heart of the principles for making every geography lesson count. Once we have planned a challenging curriculum, expertly explained difficult concepts and modelled what we want students to be able to do, they need the chance to do something with this information: to practise using it.

The aim of this practice is to ensure that students have learnt what we intended them to learn; that there has been a change in their long-term memory.[1] As such, we want to move from concentrating on the activities that students are doing towards thinking more about how we ensure that these activities lead to secure learning.

This can be difficult, as we can't necessarily control what students remember. I taught one lesson many years ago in which students spent a lot of time creating a shanty town out of cardboard boxes. Every so often they would have to deal with a challenge faced by people in settlements like these, such as clearances or flooding, and then carry on building. The idea was that they would learn about the conditions that people living in informal settlements face and the challenges they have to overcome. By the time we got to the next lesson, however, it was clear that what the students actually remembered was how to make model houses and not much else. They remembered the activity but not the content.

Another potential problem with practice occurs when it does work: when students learn from their practice, but this includes embedding their mistakes. Practice doesn't make perfect but it may make permanent.[2] You hear about this

---

1   Kirschner, Sweller and Clark, Why Minimal Guidance during Instruction Does Not Work.

2   K. Anders Ericsson, Ralf Th. Krampe and Clemens Tesch-Romer, The Role of Deliberate Practice in the Acquisition of Expert Performance, *Psychological Review* 100(3) (1993): 363–406.

when you talk to swimming coaches who spend much of their time correcting the poor form that people develop by doing lengths badly. The same thing has happened to Shaun in the example at the start of the chapter. He has been faithfully copying the same error every time he has practised drawing a climate graph to the point where this mistake is now completely embedded. Practice needs to be careful and deliberate.

There are two important aspects to practice in the geography classroom. The first is the practice of recalling information in order to strengthen this recall for the future. This is a necessary part of the learning process and ensures that our students become knowledgeable geographers. The second is the practice of producing a finished piece of work, whether an extended piece of writing – such as an investigation or decision-making task – or a geographical skill – such as presenting cartographic data or carrying out statistical tests of significance.

The following strategies consider the ways in which we can ensure that practice leads to secure learning.

1. The Testing Effect

Could weighing the pig make it grow?

We expect our students to remember a lot. Imagine you wanted to display all the key geographical terms you want them to be able to use. Is your classroom big enough? The glossaries of many GCSE textbooks run to a dozen or so pages, and these are just the tier 3 subject-specific terms that students are unlikely to encounter in everyday life. In the three-tier language model, tier 1 words are ones that come up in everyday conversation, like table or baby, and tier 2 words are those that are more specialist but cut across domains.[3] Students need to be able to recall: the difference between unfamiliar tier 3 terminology like water insecurity and water stress; the meaning of asthenosphere and lithosphere, and their characteristics; the thalweg and slip-off slope in a river; and many more intricate definitions and distinctions.

On top of becoming well-versed in a whole new vocabulary, we also need students to be able to recall a wealth of information about particular case studies and use this to support an argument. We might expect them to know that 2,000 people move to Lagos, Nigeria, each day; that the floating informal settlement there, where many people fish in the lagoon, is called Makoko; that the agency in charge of improving transport is called the Lagos Metropolitan Area Transport Authority (LAMATA), and the details of their schemes; and that they are building the Eko Atlantic development on land reclaimed from the sea.

We need to find a way to make sure that this information has been learnt and that it can be recalled when needed. Research by Roediger and Karpicke suggests that we can achieve this goal through frequent low-stakes quizzes.[4] It used to be said of testing that "weighing the pig doesn't make it grow", but research suggests that the contrary seems to be true. To strengthen recall we have to practise recall.

The simplest way to use this testing effect to improve recall is to hold a quick quiz at the start of each lesson. Prepare ten questions on one slide, with some taken from the previous lesson, some from last term and a couple from further back. The idea here is to ensure that students recall information from their long-term memory back into their working

---

3 Isabel L. Beck, Margaret G. McKeown and Linda Kucan, *Bringing Words to Life* (New York: The Guilford Press, 2002).

4 Henry L. Roediger and Jeffrey D. Karpicke, Test-Enhanced Learning: Taking Memory Tests Improves Long-Term Retention, *Psychological Science* 17(3) (2006): 249–255. Available at: https://www.ncbi.nlm.nih.gov/pubmed/16507066.

memory and so strengthen their ability to recall it in the future.[5]

Once you have chosen and written your quiz questions, put the answers on the next slide so students can quickly mark their own work. You can easily see their scores out of ten – for example, by asking them to hold up the number of fingers to correspond to how many they got right or by reading out each question and asking for hands up for a correct answer. You can also use these results to identify any areas that need reteaching (see Chapter 5, there is an example of such a quiz in on page 101).

They can also practise recall through self-testing; a method of study found to be particularly effective in the research compiled by John Dunlosky.[6] When students study at home they tend to avoid activities that involve thinking hard and favour methods that feel comfortable, such as highlighting or rereading notes. These methods don't require them to recall information because it is sat there in front of them. Instead, we should encourage them to:

♦ **Draw mind maps of a topic from memory.** This allows them to see what they can recall, before checking to see what they need to add, as well as enabling them to practise making links between different parts of the topic.

♦ **Create flashcards**. They can create a bank of cards with questions on one side and answers on the other and work through the stack. If they get the question wrong, it stays in the stack; if they get it right, they can put it to one side for now. This has the added advantage of revealing the areas of a topic that they need to spend more time revising.

---

5   For more on what is known as the Ebbinghaus Forgetting Curve see: Carolina Kuepper-Tetzel, Optimizing Your Learning Schedule, *The Learning Scientists* [blog] (5 July 2018). Available at: http://www.learningscientists.org/blog/2018/7/5-1?rq=Ebbinghaus.

6   John Dunlosky, Strengthening the Student Toolbox: Study Strategies to Boost Learning, *American Educator* 37(3) (2013): 12–21. Available at: https://www.aft.org/sites/default/files/periodicals/dunlosky.pdf.

♦ **Draw diagrams.** Geographical study is full of diagrams. Students can use the study-cover-reproduce-check strategy to ensure that they know the steps involved in the creation of a spit or the location of informal housing in Lagos, for example.

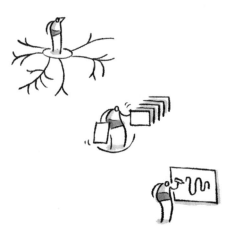

2. Look Both Ways

How can we ensure recall happens during the lesson?

Although a quiz at the start of the lesson is a great way to practise recalling key information, it can be devoid of context. What sets geography apart from other subjects is the value placed on building links between different topics, on thinking like a geographer and on seeing the connections between the different parts of our broad subject. These links between topics create natural points at which to revisit previous lessons and use the information in a new context.

For example, as part of the GCSE course you might study Nigeria as an example of an LIC or NEE with a focus on its rapid economic development. This could involve looking at Nigeria's equatorial climate on the coast and the reasons why it becomes more arid as you move further north. This in turn would allow you to revisit the issues surrounding desertification and water security. If you had looked at Lagos earlier in the course, as a case study on the impact of urbanisation or the challenges of urban spaces, you could revisit this example and contrast the economic development of Lagos with that of Kano in the north of the country.

There is no reason why this has to be limited within a key stage either. I am not suggesting that we teach a five-year GCSE course, but rather that we conceive of students' learning as a thirteen-year course running right from the start of their academic education until the end. You may only be responsible for a section of this but it certainly helps to know what came before and what will come after it. Obviously this would involve a lot of central planning and work with feeder primary schools to be made a reality. Within secondary schools, the focus on linking the key stages together can help to combat what Ofsted terms the "wasted years" of Key Stage 3. They wrote that:

"Inspectors observed MFL, history and geography lessons at Key Stage 3 in 51 routine inspections carried out during June and July 2015. Inspectors reported significant weaknesses in all three subjects. Too often, inspectors found teaching that failed to challenge and engage pupils."[7]

We need to plan our geography curriculum carefully and make the links between content explicit at every opportunity. We also need to make it clear that students are not expected to do tasks just for the sake of completing them;

---

7   Ofsted, *Key Stage 3: The Wasted Years?* Reference no: 150106 (September 2015). Available at: https://www.gov.uk/government/publications/key-stage-3-the-wasted-years, p. 5.

they need to learn the content and be able to recall it in the future. This means looking forward as well as back, and explaining to students how they will be able to use what they are learning. For this to be effective, we need to plan out a clear curriculum with this principle in mind.

To make these connections explicit we can:

♦ Provide students with a topic overview showing what they will study that year and how it links to other areas they have studied or will go on to study.

♦ Use knowledge quizzes at the start of lessons, including questions from previous topics that link to the current area of study. We can explain these links as we go through the answers.

♦ Ask the students themselves to make links between the topics. Arrange the topics in a circle – on a piece of paper or displayed on the board – and ask them to draw lines to show the connections between them, writing what the connection is along the line. This can also be a useful revision task, as they need to think hard about what they have studied.

♦ Turn the idea above into a corridor display showing the big picture of what will be studied and how it all connects together. In this way, we are making the thinking of a geographer very visible.

♦ Make links explicit through questioning. For example, when studying the urban challenges in London we might ask if Lagos would have the same priorities, or what role climate or deindustrialisation might play in these issues.

3. Micro-Details

Do we learn from doing drills?

If you were planning to run a marathon, would you head out the door to run 26.2 miles on the first day of training, then go out the next day to repeat the same distance but slightly faster, then do the same again on day three and so on? I'd certainly hope not. It takes time and practice to prepare your body for such a challenge without risking significant discomfort and injury. If you want to get better at something, you practise its component parts and improve each aspect. So instead, you might head out for one long run at the weekend and slowly build up your distance, do some short fast runs during the week, and perhaps do some strength training as well. Proponents of ChiRunning would suggest that before you even lace up your trainers you should spend some time getting your form right with carefully constructed drills designed to work on posture and strengthen the foot.[8] We can apply this same approach to practice in the classroom.

If we want to make better geographers, should we just ask students to practise being geographers? Should we set them up with a detailed geographical enquiry to work through, for instance? We could give them an area to explore, such as

---

8   See https://www.chirunning.com/.

crime patterns in our neighbourhood, let them come up with their enquiry questions, set a hypothesis, write about the theory they are exploring, collect data through primary and secondary sources, decide how to display and analyse that data, reach a conclusion and evaluate their study. This certainly sounds very engaging and challenging.

The problem with trying to get better at geography by practising being geographers is that students don't yet have the knowledge and skills with which to practise effectively. The type of enquiry described above is similar to the work we would expect an A level student to complete at the end of thirteen years of careful study; it is an end we are working towards rather than a means of delivering the content. If we jump in to this kind of independent enquiry too soon, we run the risk that students' practice will be embedding errors and that learning will be superficial, as they haven't been taught the subject in enough depth to make it meaningful.

Instead, we need students to practise the component parts of being a geographer. They need to be shown various different methods for displaying and interpreting geographical data and work with them in various contexts; they need repeated opportunities to reach conclusions and to justify them with reference to evidence; and they need to evaluate their findings with reference to reliability and validity.

The idea of drills has got something of an image problem, as people picture students endlessly copying out lines or chanting in response to a didactic teacher. When we talk about a drill though, all we mean is that students practise smaller components of a task until they have mastered a skill. This could involve:

♦ Describing distribution on a choropleth map.

♦ Carrying out a cost-benefit analysis.

♦ Understanding the term "sustainable development".

♦ Writing the opening sentence to answer a question giving their assessment of a plan.

♦ Using evidence from an Ordnance Survey (OS) map in decision-making.

All these examples will benefit from plenty of deliberate practice after effective explanation and modelling. Once students have mastered the tools of the geographer's trade they are ready to use them to *do* geography.

4. Return to Fertile Questions

Isn't the whole greater than the sum of its parts?

Although students need to develop skills and knowledge in small deliberate steps, they also need the opportunity to put it all together. In Chapter 1, I discussed the idea of planning the curriculum around what Knight and Benson term "fertile questions", questions that explore students' deep conceptual understanding of our subject. In geography, we tend to think of this way of approaching the subject as "enquiry".

Research by Margaret Roberts has found that the term "enquiry" means different things to different teachers.[9] Over the years it has been heavily associated with constructivism in education, such that enquiry is almost seen as synonymous with project-based learning.[10] It is important that we, as geography teachers, are able to redefine the term for our subject as it is an important aspect in "thinking geographically".

---

9 Margaret Roberts, *Geography through Enquiry: Approaches to Teaching and Learning in the Secondary School* (Sheffield: Geographical Association, 2013).

10 The idea of "geographical enquiry" was born out of the Schools Council geography projects from the 1970s and 1980s and was heavily influenced by the work of Piaget, Vygotsky and Brunner and the idea that students need to "construct" their own understanding by building on ideas they already have.

Roberts suggests that enquiry has four characteristics:

♦ It is driven by questions – including a questioning of received knowledge.

♦ It uses evidence and examples from the real world.

♦ It asks students to think geographically and to develop a conceptual understanding of the subject.

♦ It encourages students to reflect on what they have learnt.

Roberts also justifies the use of enquiry with four arguments:[11]

♦ A constructivist approach suggests students need to build on what they already know and construct their own understanding of a topic.

♦ Enquiry enables them to think geographically about an issue and form deeper conceptual understanding.

♦ It is important for developing twenty-first-century skills.

♦ It is a requirement for GCSE and A level.

However, enquiry-based learning does not need to be seen as incompatible with a more traditional or knowledge-based approach. Roberts also suggests that enquiry does not need to involve long-term open-ended projects but would fit into a much more tightly structured one or two hours of learning.

At its heart, enquiry-based learning should involve setting powerful, or fertile, questions and teaching students the knowledge and providing them with the real-world geographical information to answer them. Students may critique this information – by GCSE they will need to challenge the usefulness of data, for example – and they may also start to filter and select examples that they feel are more relevant to the question. However, this can only come with time and teaching.

---

11 Roberts, Planning for Enquiry.

If we return to the example from Strategy 3, micro-details, we could start with the fertile question, "Which geographical factors influence crime rates in our neighbourhood?" We could then teach students the theories that help to explain spatial variations in crime rates, explore crime statistics and how to interpret them, model ways of displaying this data, and then use exemplars to show what a finished enquiry write-up might look like (for more on exemplars see Chapter 3). They could then answer the fertile question using what they have learnt.

By framing a topic as a fertile question, students are taught to link together different pieces of relevant knowledge and to draw on things they have learnt in the past. They approach a topic as a geographer and develop a conceptual understanding of the whole rather than a more fragmented view of the discipline as a series of small, unconnected parts.

5. Functional Fitness

Should we be practising for the exam?

Sadly, when teachers talk about practice it is usually in the context of exams. There are things we can, and should, do to prepare students for important exams but there is no better preparation than teaching them well.

One reason why exam practice is so fraught with difficulty in our subject is that so many marks are awarded for the application of knowledge to unpredictable questions. In Strategy 3, I used the analogy of running to show how we might train to improve our fitness and ability over distance. The problem with marathon running is that it only makes you good at one thing: marathon running. It is very hard to take what you have learnt about distance running, and the fitness you have developed through it, and use it to help you swim or lift something heavy. This is where the idea of functional fitness comes in. Functional fitness programs, such as CrossFit, stress that we need to train in a way that makes us ready for anything, by including a lot of varied and unpredictable practice.

We can apply this analogy to teaching geography. If students practise specific past exam questions then there is a danger that we are just preparing them to answer those questions – questions that are unlikely to come up again. This approach also leaves them unprepared to take geography further at A level and university, and doesn't deepen their real-life geographical understanding.

If we look at a GCSE geography exam specification, we often see a list of content that we need to deliver. For example, the AQA specification calls for a case study on an LIC or NEE that is going through rapid economic development. It then gives a list of things students should know about this case study – for example, the changing employment structure, the impact on the environment, the role of TNCs and so on. We could, in theory, teach this as an extended fact file of information that they need to be able to recall. While it is certainly true that they will need to recall a lot of specific information, this approach wouldn't create the deeper understanding of the place that would allow them to apply their knowledge to whichever questions they are asked. It would leave them unprepared.

Instead, we need to look beyond the exam questions and the specification to explore the underlying geography. If I chose Nigeria as a case study, I might consider the following questions:

♦ What barriers to development has Nigeria had to overcome?

♦ Why hasn't everyone benefited from the rapid development in Nigeria?

♦ What role have outsiders, from the British Empire to TNCs, played in Nigeria's development?

If you have taught your students well enough for them to give confident answers to these questions, and ones like them, then they should have no difficulty with whatever the exam asks.

Where students might benefit from focused exam-specific practice is around the language of the questions. Students need to understand what the different command words mean and how they should approach answering these different types of questions, including when and how to use sources of information. We can demonstrate this through exemplars and live modelling (see Chapter 3). They also need to understand how to use the number of marks on offer for different questions as a guide to dividing their time.

Beyond these few simple strategies, I would suggest that we remember that, fundamentally, the exam paper is designed to assess what students have learnt from the curriculum. We shouldn't allow the exam to *become* the curriculum by focusing all our time and attention on practising for it. We practise because it enables us to learn; we don't learn to enable us to practise.

6. Support and Self-Regulation

How much help should we give during practice?

There is a natural tension between our desire to see what students are able to do by themselves and the need to intervene to make sure that they are getting it right. This tension exists, at least in part, because of a confusion between practice and performance.

When students are "performing" they are putting together what they have learnt and producing something with it. This might be a piece of extended writing, an analysis of geographical data or simply a list of correct definitions of geographical vocabulary. We want them to carry out this performance so that we can assess what they know, under-stand and can do, and can adapt our teaching accordingly. This is very different, however, from practice.

When students are practising, they are doing it to learn – or to consolidate their learning about – something new. It is therefore important that this practice is correct, or quickly corrected, so that errors do not become embedded. As I said in the introduction to this chapter, practice doesn't make perfect but it does make permanent.

For this reason, we want to ensure that we give the right amount of support during practice. Much of this support will come from circulating the room, checking students' work as they are producing it and looking for common errors that need immediate correction. Over time, teachers collect a mental list of typical kinds of error: not labelling axes on a graph, discussing the hole in the ozone layer in relation to climate change, assuming that sustainability is only about the environment and so on. These errors are often very specific to each topic. By being aware of these areas of misunderstanding, we can pre-empt them and inter-vene appropriately.

A lot of this support will come from the strategies discussed in the chapters on explanation and modelling. We might support students' practice with exemplar answers to similar questions, by leaving notes on the board for them to refer to or by giving them success criteria to use as they work. That final idea of using success criteria can be especially powerful as it helps us to reach one of the goal endpoints of educa-tion: self-regulation.

Self-regulation is the ability of students to reflect on their own work and make improvements to it. As with the ability to independently run a geographical enquiry, it is something that we are working towards rather than something we would expect students to be able to do from the start. We will consider the role of self-regulation more in Chapter 5. In the meantime, here are a few techniques that we can use to help develop their self-regulation over time:

♦ Create success criteria as a class so that students understand what makes an excellent piece of geographical work. It is also important that they can see how the criteria varies according to the task.

♦ Ask students to proofread their own work and check it against the success criteria before showing it to the teacher. We might ask them to make a certain number of basic corrections before we agree to read it and offer more substantial feedback.

♦ Use peer assessment so that they get used to looking for the strengths and weaknesses in each other's work. It is sometimes easier to identify this in someone else's work than in your own.

♦ Encourage students to use self-testing to practise recall but also to work out the gaps they have in their knowledge. Over time, they can start to take more responsibility and plan how they will close these gaps.

Many teachers have embraced the central place of practice as outlined in *Making Every Lesson Count*. The following case study from Tom Highnett explains how his department approach this aspect of teaching.

Case Study: Practice

Tom Highnett, head of humanities, Outwood Academy Foxhills

When it comes to practice, I have tried to introduce two distinct strategies. The first of these involves the use of regular quizzes. In my lessons, we tend to cover a lot of content – specific facts, concepts, theories, case studies and so on – and these are underpinned by a broad base of knowledge. To ensure that students become fluent with this content, we start every lesson with a quiz. This takes the form of ten questions on the whiteboard, which students complete independently. These quizzes comprise five questions from the current topic and five questions from past topics – to encourage revision of prior content.

The quiz is timed – and when the time is up, answers are shared and students self-assess. I circulate during this process and ensure that students are completing their quiz and self-assessing properly.

Second, students are given lots of opportunities to practise their written work, which always involves the application of new knowledge. To take an example, my GCSE students will practise exam questions, usually the 6–9-mark questions, which involve them writing for an extended period of time and, often, making an argument. To support students in completing this, I will initially provide a model paragraph – which is shared in full and dissected with a particular focus on what's good and what could be improved. Using the notes from our class discussion, students practise writing their own paragraphs. The key here is emphasising that this is *practice* – we are trying to apply what we have just learnt from the model paragraph – for example, the use of facts, linking back to the question or presenting an argument. By creating small-scale, focused opportunities for practice, students can drill these skills regularly before approaching an exam question as one solid task.

This process of modelling and practice requires constant planning, especially when introducing a change of topic or new content. Practice is only effective when students have a strong knowledge base on which to draw, which is why we work so hard to combine regular quizzing with the application of knowledge.

Chapter 5
Feedback

Miss Jones

Every Friday, Miss Jones loads up her bag with exercise books and drags them down the corridor and out to her car. From her car, they make their way into her hall, where she spends the weekend tripping over them as they sit there in silent reproach. When it comes to Sunday evening, with a heavy heart, she sits in front of the TV with a red pen in hand and faithfully works through her marking piles. She reads through the students' work and adds useful comments like "include an example" and "don't forget to build towards a conclusion". If she looked further back in their books she would see that she has been writing the same comments every Sunday night, all year.

Gary

Gary gets his book back on Monday morning ready for some dedicated improvement and reflection time (DIRT). There is a big display board behind him spelling this out, alongside examples of student work, but he stopped noticing it about one minute after it went up. He looks at the comments on his work; yet again they ask him to include an example and build towards a conclusion. "If I knew how to build towards a conclusion I would," he thinks, as he doodles in the margin.

The fact that feedback is important for learning is a truth almost universally acknowledged. Going back to our running example from the previous chapter, it would be useful to have a coach who can give you feedback on your form so that you can then do specific drills to strengthen muscles that show weakness. When cooking a dish for the first time, it helps to get feedback on how it is coming together by tasting it so that you can make adjustments. When learning to drive, it helps to have feedback on things like your road positioning so that you can adjust it the next time you are making a similar manoeuvre. We look for feedback from various sources all the time, including experts and our own instincts, so that we can improve. As teachers we also receive feedback on how our students are progressing and on their particular strengths, weaknesses and any gaps in their knowledge. As such we can see that feedback has a dual purpose.

The Education Endowment Foundation (EEF) recognises the significant role that feedback plays in the classroom. Their analysis of the evidence around its impact suggests that effective feedback could lead to eight months of additional progress for students.[1] This is more than with any other form of intervention. However, the EEF also notes that although many studies show the highly positive impact of feedback, there are also studies that reveal how feedback can have a *negative* impact on progress. If the wrong feedback is given, students make less progress than they would otherwise have made.

---

1 See https://educationendowmentfoundation.org.uk/evidence-summaries/ teaching-learning-toolkit/feedback/.

One reason why feedback might sometimes backfire is because it needs to be used in different ways at different times, and this can be easy to misjudge. Hattie and Timperley explain that feedback about a specific task is often best given immediately after completion to correct errors and misconceptions. However, feedback about the process of the work, or feedback about how the student is managing their own learning – their self-regulation – is often best delayed. It could be that teachers are providing these kinds of feedback at the wrong time.[2]

Another problem with feedback is that it can be incredibly time-consuming, a problem that has been highlighted by the Department for Education's working group on teacher workload, who comment that:

> *"Marking has evolved into an unhelpful burden for teachers, when the time it takes is not repaid in positive impact on pupils' progress. This is frequently because it is serving a different purpose such as demonstrating teacher performance or to satisfy the requirements of other, mainly adult, audiences."* [3]

Dylan Wiliam also makes the point that feedback often takes a higher proportion of teachers' time than it should. There is always an opportunity cost and the time spent giving feedback is time taken away from planning lessons. He suggests, "teachers should be spending twice as much time on planning teaching as they do on marking".[4] In order to make

2 John Hattie and Helen Timperley, The Power of Feedback, *Review of Educational Research* 77(1) (2007): 81–112. Available at: http://education.qld. gov.au/staff/development/performance/resources/readings/power-feedback.pdf.

3 Marking Policy Review Group, *Eliminating Unnecessary Workload Around Marking: Report of the Independent Teacher Workload Review Group* (London: Department for Education, 2016). Available at: https://www.gov.uk/government/publications/reducing-teacher-workload-marking-policy-review-group-report, p. 6.

4 Dylan Wiliam, Assessment, Marking and Feedback. In Carl Hendrick and Robin MacPherson, *What Does This Look Like in the Classroom? Bridging the Gap Between Research and Practice* (Woodbridge: John Catt Educational, 2017), pp. 27–44 at p. 33.

every geography lesson count we need to use feedback in an effective and efficient way.

This chapter considers the strategies that we can use in the geography classroom to provide this kind of meaningful feedback to our students.

1. Put Down the Pen

What is the difference between marking and feedback?

One of the biggest issues with feedback is that it has become associated with just one form, that of written comments on students' work. One of the reasons for this is that it serves the purpose highlighted in the Department for Education's workload report regarding demonstrating teacher performance. Written marking is easily observed and therefore easily monitored. However, it is not necessarily the best form of feedback, for several reasons.

Improving the work

One problem with marking work in this way is that it encourages us to correct the work rather than the student. Dylan Wiliam explains that "too many teachers focus on the purpose of feedback as changing or improving the work, whereas the major purpose of feedback should be to improve the student".[5]

If I think back over the comments I have written in students' books over the years, they have tended to be about that particular piece of work – often concerning additional information students need to add. Comments on a piece of work might include:

♦ Don't forget to include an example of the economic impact of an earthquake on an LIC.

♦ Have you confused primary and secondary impacts?

♦ Include the death toll of the Nepal earthquake.

♦ Could you consider whether it is always true that primary effects are worse than secondary effects?

These comments are all very useful in getting the student to write a better answer to the question, "Assess the extent to which the primary effects of a tectonic hazard are worse than the secondary effects", but are going to be of little use to them when it comes to answering any other question. It has improved the work but not the student.

How do I build towards a conclusion?

There is also a problem if we go the other way and try to write generic comments that could be applied to a greater range of questions. On this same piece of work, I could have written:

♦ Include examples.

♦ Be clear on your definitions.

♦ Include specific facts and figures.

♦ Build towards a stronger conclusion.

---

5 Wiliam, Assessment, Marking and Feedback, p. 29.

These things would certainly apply to an array of geographical questions, but would lead to the problem that Gary had in the introduction to this chapter. They are things that most students would do if they knew how. Writing these instructions doesn't give them enough information about how to actually follow them.

Motivation

For feedback to be effective it has to be received in the right way, leading to a student believing that they can make the necessary improvements and make progress. One problem with written comments on work is that they can send the message that the piece simply isn't good enough, without providing the kind of reassurance that we would likely offer when giving this feedback verbally.

Time budget

Finally, there is the issue around time. Time is a finite resource and should be budgeted just like anything else. Opening thirty books, reading a couple of pages of each student's work and writing five or six comments on each piece takes a good couple of hours. That is time that could be spent planning a lesson to address the problems students have with their work, creating resources or improving your own subject knowledge. It has a cost.

The rest of this chapter discusses ways of giving feedback in a much more time-efficient manner, and looks at alternative approaches to feedback to help tackle the four areas of concern outlined above.

2. Whole-Class Feedback

Why might we want to give the same feedback to the whole class?

How often have you written the same handful of comments in every single book? Frequent offenders in geography are:

♦ Add more detail.

♦ Explain your point.

♦ Include evidence.

♦ So?

This is one reason why we might be better off using whole-class feedback (WCF); it allows us to comment on those common errors that many students are making and show them how to do things differently.

When I am using WCF, I will look through a pile of work and make notes about frequently occurring mistakes or areas for improvement. I also take a photo of any examples of excellent work. The next lesson, students get their books back and I talk them through the common errors, which they look for in their own work. This helps to develop their self-regulation. This is important as I can't always be there to provide feedback on their work – I certainly won't be in the exam – and they need to become adept at spotting errors for themselves.

During this session, I will show them the photos of excellent work with an added commentary about why it is of the standard that I am expecting. I can also reteach any misconceptions that featured in their work, as well as giving exemplars to illustrate these points (see Chapter 3). In the tectonic hazards example, this might include the difference between primary and secondary impacts and details of the Nepal earthquake.

Importantly, students must now do something with the feedback they have been given. Sometimes it is useful for them to apply the feedback to the original piece of work, if redrafting it will lead to more secure learning of the key knowledge or processes. More often, though, it is useful to set a second task to address the issues raised. This could be a second question that covers similar ideas but with a different focus – for example, "Assess the extent to which the primary effects of *tropical storms* are more significant than the secondary effects" – or shorter questions that address the particular issues identified. For the tectonic hazards example, this might include:

1 Give three primary and three secondary effects of a tectonic hazard.

2 Rank all six in order of significance.

3 Why might the primary effects be more significant for LICs than HICs?

4 How does Nepal help to show this?

This type of feedback takes less time than marking a set of books – and becomes quicker the more you do it. Furthermore, it addresses the issue of improving students' transferable skills rather than a specific piece of work, through the use of exemplars and by giving students very specific things to work on in response to the feedback. This approach also makes the critique feel less personal; it is clear that you are making improvements as a class, and students are each finding and correcting their mistakes with your support.

3. Personal Review

Why might we need to give feedback to students one-to-one?

There are of course times when we do want feedback to be more personal. As we have discussed, feedback on a task is often best given live, as students are completing the work, as we want to pick up any misconceptions before they become embedded. This also means that students can act on the feedback immediately to improve their current work. When you spot a problem, there are three approaches you could take:

♦ Tell the student what mistake they have made and how to correct it. This might be a spelling or grammatical error or a factual mistake in their work.

♦ Place a dot in the margin near the error and ask them to find it. This asks them to practise reviewing their work and looking for improvements.

♦ Stop the lesson. If you have come across the same problem in a number of students' work then it probably means that you need to go over something again. This might be a mistake in how to draw a certain type of graph or cartographic display or how to structure an in-depth answer. This mass misunderstanding tends to indicate a need to re-model or reteach what they need to do before they try again (see Chapter 3).

It is also useful to plan in time to sit with each student to give them detailed verbal feedback on their work. When the rest of the class are working quietly on a task, sit with one student and look through their work over the previous few weeks. This allows you to look at and discuss the progress they are making over time rather than focusing on individual pieces of work.

You might notice that a student often fails to include enough detail in their work, or struggles to justify their conclusions. Rather than leaving them with a comment that they don't know what to do with, like Gary at the start of this chapter, you have the chance to talk about what this should look like and even work on it with them there and then. This kind of detailed one-to-one coaching just can't be replicated with written comments on a student's work. Even if you only get to sit down with each student three times a year, the impact of these discussions can be very powerful.

The powerful effect of immediate feedback is noted by Rosenshine in his Principles of Instruction.[6] He explains that students need regular opportunities to review the work that they have done and to make links between different topics. As they work, they are developing their schemata; their mental maps of the subject. By sitting with them and discussing their work, we have the opportunity to explore these links. As we saw in Chapter 3, the curse of knowledge can mean that the links between lessons that seem so obvious to us will be hidden from students unless we make them explicit.

A recent one-to-one review I carried out with a Year 11 student covered the following:

♦ Their work on the Nepal earthquake. Their understanding of the problems with building quality in the capital was a little simplistic. We discussed this and linked it to their work on population pressures and the demographic transition model.

---

6   Rosenshine, Principles of Instruction.

♦ How they had a habit of writing everything they knew about a case study in answer to a question rather than using specifics to make a point. I modelled how to use examples to support a point and set them a short task to develop this ability.

♦ As we were talking, it became clear that while their knowledge was good, they were struggling to see the links between different pieces of information and with how to use what they knew to answer a question. We looked at how they could revise in a way that focused more on the application of knowledge.

Even doing this review with just one student can help you to identify wider issues that might exist in the whole class, and this insight allows you to respond and adapt your teaching (see Strategy 5).

4. Peer Pressure

Is peer feedback the blind leading the blind?

One barrier to overcome when giving effective feedback is simply a matter of numbers. In each lesson you can have over thirty students all looking for feedback from just one teacher. A solution can of course be to use peer feedback, by getting the students to read and comment on each other's work. It is worth being a little cautious here and reminding ourselves of the dual purpose of feedback mentioned at the start of this chapter:

♦ To find out what a student knows, understands and can do.

♦ To let them know what they need to do next.

The first issue with peer feedback is that you, as a teacher, miss the opportunity to review what students have learnt and check on their progress. The second issue is that the student giving the feedback may have little idea about what success looks like or what their peer needs to do to improve. Teachers receive, or should receive, a lot of training in giving meaningful feedback. It is hardly surprising that peer feedback is difficult to get right, as students will also need this training experience.

Often, peer feedback sessions involve students reading each other's work and writing a comment to identify successes – what went well (WWW) – and targets for improvement – even better if (EBI). I have lost count of the number of WWWs I've seen that read something like:

Really good.

Very neat.

Well written.

And EBIs that say:

Hard to read your handwriting.

Need to write more.

Give more detail.

These comments from peer feedback share all the problematic features that we discussed in relation to teachers' written comments; they are too generic and don't give meaningful direction. However, we can make peer feedback work; we just need to make sure that students are coached in what makes feedback constructive and actionable.

First, make sure that the person giving the feedback has very clear success criteria in mind and, preferably, an exemplar piece for comparison. Give some prompts to help shape meaningful feedback. For a decision-making task this might be:

♦ Have they discussed the role of different stakeholders?

♦ Have they discussed whether the scheme is sustainable?

♦ Have they mentioned economic, social and environmental factors?

- ◆ Have they referred to specific evidence?

- ◆ Does the conclusion match what they have argued in the rest of the piece?

It also helps to change the focus slightly and make the process useful for the person giving the feedback as well as for the recipient. Once a student has given feedback, ask them to reflect back on their own work. Is theirs more or less successful than the piece they have looked at? Why? Can they justify this with reference to the success criteria? Have they made any of the same mistakes? Were there any good points in the piece they looked at that they would now like to include in their own work?

This combination of peer feedback followed by self-assessment can lead to a much deeper reflection about what makes a good piece of geographical work and more opportunities for students to apply what they have learnt in practice.

5. Responsive Teaching

What role does feedback play during the lesson itself?

The focus on written comments as the primary form of feedback has encouraged us to look at feedback as something that happens at a distinct point in time, which is a problematic view. The recent move towards structuring time for students to respond to feedback in DIRT sessions has been useful in putting the emphasis back on what students actually do with the feedback their teachers have taken the time to give. Nevertheless, the idea continues that feedback just happens at a certain point in the lesson.

We need to remember that feedback is a constant process and that it works both ways: informing both teacher and students. When students do a quick quiz at the start of the lesson they receive immediate feedback about what they know and about the gaps in their knowledge, and so do we. When students have marked their answers, ask them to put up their hands if they got them right as you run through the correct answers. This gives a quick indication of any areas that need reteaching and allows you to respond to address knowledge gaps.

This response can take many forms, depending on the nature of the gap. If it is a common misconception, it can quickly be addressed there and then – for example, homelessness is a secondary effect of an earthquake, rainforests have nutrient-rich soil, or China is a HIC. Addressing these errors as soon as students have made them helps the correct information to stick.[7]

---

7 Pooja K. Agarwal, Patrice M. Bain and Roger W. Chamberlain, The Value of Applied Research: Retrieval Practice Improves Classroom Learning and Recommendations from a Teacher, a Principal and a Scientist, *Education Psychology Review* 24 (2012): 437–448.

Another way to tackle these gaps could be through homework. It would only take a moment to devise a series of tasks to deepen and test knowledge areas that seem to be lacking. Assign an exploratory task to each of the quiz questions and get the students to complete it if they got that question wrong. This could look something like the following.

Testing knowledge with tasks

1 Name the three processes carried out by waves.

   Task: Draw a diagram to illustrate each of the processes.

2 On which type of coastline to you tend to find headlands and bays?

   Task: Describe the landforms on the Dorset coast and explain why Swanage Bay is found where it is.

3 What impact will the building of groynes have on beaches further east on the Dorset coast?

   Task: Draw a diagram showing how groynes prevent longshore drift.

Sometimes quizzing, or other forms of assessment, reveals a more significant difficulty that the whole class is having that needs to be addressed by reteaching. This doesn't mean running the same lesson again but rather adding something new to help them make sense of what they have previously covered. For example, in a Year 13 lesson I noticed that students hadn't really understood the equation showing the risk level from a tectonic hazard. They had looked at case studies on Nepal and Japan but were struggling to explain the different factors that created risk in those countries. They had focused on levels of development but hadn't really grasped the idea that seismic hazards present in different ways or the differences between vulnerability and coping capacity.

Rather than simply reteaching these case studies, I shared a third example with them. We looked at the Haiti earthquake and explored the physical hazards, the country's level of vulnerability and its capacity to cope. I worked through an annotated copy of the risk equation for Haiti and then students applied these insights to annotate copies for Nepal and Japan.

We need to recognise feedback as an intrinsic part of every lesson. When we are sharing examples of excellence and asking students to adapt their own work as a result, we are giving feedback. We are giving feedback when we ask questions and then use follow-up questioning to dig deeper or ask students to rephrase their answers. We are giving feedback when we stop at a student's desk and adapt our teaching to meet their needs. At its heart, both good learning and good teaching is about responding to feedback.

6. Building Self-Regulation

Can we take the teacher out of the feedback process?

Ultimately, we want to get to the point where students are able to monitor their own learning, reflect on what they have done and act on this reflection. They are not going to have a teacher by their side throughout their life, or in an exam, and so ultimately need to take charge of their own learning without us. This is where metacognition and self-regulation become important.

As Alex Quigley and Eleanor Stringer explain, "An effective learner will monitor their knowledge and cognitive processes, and use this understanding to make judgements about how to direct their efforts."[8] They are very clear that this metacognitive ability needs to be taught and that it needs to be taught alongside specific subjects rather than as a generic "thinking skill". We can't think about our learning without having something to think *about*.

There are a number of ways in which we can encourage self-regulation and teach metacognition so students learn to take more responsibility for acting on feedback. Here are a few examples:

- **Review first.** Encourage students to get into the habit of reviewing their work before asking the teacher to look at it. Insist that they make at least one correction or improvement themselves.

- **Get unstuck.** Students often ask for feedback on a task because they are feeling stuck. They need to develop a range of strategies to get themselves unstuck without resorting to the teacher.

  ◊ If they don't understand a particular word, they can cover it up and see if the sentence makes sense without it. Can they now decipher the meaning of the word?

  ◊ Can they look back at a similar task to see for themselves what they need to do to get started? This can work particularly well for the perennial problem of students not knowing how to start a paragraph.

  ◊ Think like a geographer. There are common ways in which a geographer approaches a problem or a

---

8 Alex Quigley and Eleanor Stringer, Making Sense of Metacognition, *Impact: Journal of the Chartered College of Teaching* 3 (2018): 26–30. Available at: https://impact.chartered.college/article/quigley-stringer-making-sense-metacognition/.

decision-making task. Can they think about it in terms of economic, social and environmental issues? Local, national or global ones? Long- or short-term concerns? Having these common structures in mind makes it easier to start a task.

♦ **Model metacognition.** When modelling live (see Chapter 3) we can also model metacognition strategies. Think aloud and show how you are regulating your own thought processes and adapting what you write as a result – for example, "I'm not sure where to go next with this … I'm thinking that if I try …"

♦ **Rewind.** Encourage the class to look back over their books since the beginning of the year to see for themselves how their work is improving. Get them to identify what they know now that they didn't at the start and what they can do now that they couldn't then.

In the fast pace of the classroom we can struggle to make time for students to reflect on their learning and build their capacity to cope when they run into difficulties. We need to find this time if we are going to develop learners who can eventually continue their journey without us. In the following case study, Paul Logue explains how he has persevered with getting his students to take responsibility for feedback.

Case Study: Feedback

Paul Logue, subject leader for Key Stage 5, Debden Park High School

It's hard to think of a topic as marmite as the use and merits of peer and self-assessment. I must admit I am a new convert, having tried many forms of it previously and having had a lack of success stories. My use of it has evolved over time and I have dismissed many approaches that are linked to teaching myths about what will be effective: two stars and a wish went in my NQT year, WWW and EBI in my RQT year and so on. The fault with many of these strategies is that they are used primarily in order to meet a marking policy requirement and fail to assess students' actual understanding. Students need targets that match their development needs, and these devices do not represent a holistic and structured approach to address the knowledge they have and lack.

My faith has been restored thanks to excellent CPD led by a former colleague and lead practitioner, Lindsay Underwood, that has encouraged me to be more mindful and exploratory with the strategies I incorporate. A huge inspiration has been Dylan Wiliam's "four quarters marking", which has really assisted me in giving purposeful feedback and monitoring high-quality work.[9] Now I embrace wonderful and varied feedback methods – such as WCF, visualiser marking, live marking and a new favourite, Keep It, Bin It, Build It – in order to ensure students are developing their work professionally and writing like geographers. Keep It, Bin It, Build It allows students – either self-reflectively or through peer marking – to highlight or colour-code their writing against the success criteria, scrutinising what is excellent (Keep It), information that is not relevant to the answer (Bin It) and areas that require further development (Build It). Students have embraced this method really well and have become more considerate about their writing as a result.

---

9   Wiliam, Assessment, Marking and Feedback, p. 32.

Chapter 6

Questioning

Mr Johnson

"Good morning, class. We are going to start a new topic on Ghana. Can anyone tell me the capital of Ghana? Yes, Shane … London? No, Shane, London is the capital of England. Anyone else? Yes, Tyler … You have been to London? That is very interesting but I was asking about the capital of Ghana. Yes, Emma … You want to add to what Tyler was saying? But I was asking about the capital of Ghana. OK class, I'll give you a clue. It starts with an A and rhymes with Daccra ..."

Monique

Monique is sat low in her chair trying to avoid the teacher's eye. The class are being asked about the formation of different landforms and the types of erosion involved. Monique didn't know there were different types of erosion, never mind how they lead to different landforms. Luckily, she knows that if she keeps her head down she won't be asked and won't have to make it obvious that the lesson is passing her by.

Watch almost any teacher at work and you will see them ask a barrage of questions. Some to the class, some directed at small groups and others at pairs. Questioning is a vital part of any lesson; indeed, Rosenshine found that effective teachers ask significantly more questions than less effective ones.[1] Its importance in the geography classroom is perhaps even more apparent: ours is a questioning discipline. Geographers ask questions about the world and then gather the information they need to form a conclusion. When we ask questions as geography teachers, we are not only deploying a pedagogical tool but are modelling an aspect of our subject.

In general, teachers ask questions for three main reasons: to check for understanding, to improve recall and to deepen thinking. Because we want questioning to serve different purposes, it is important that we consider the point of each question, or questioning session, and approach it in the best way.

One precondition that is important regardless is to ensure that you have developed a culture of questioning in your classroom. A culture of questioning is one in which asking questions is valued and students feel comfortable trying to answer them. They need to know that you appreciate when they ask good geographical questions and that they won't be dismissed or ignored. When a student does ask a particularly insightful question, it is worth using the school's reward system to celebrate it. Also important is to explain to the class why you consider this an especially good question. For example, does it:

♦ Show a link to learning from a previous lesson?

♦ Draw on their own general knowledge or wider reading?

♦ Include a good use of geographical language?

♦ Suggest a problem or solution that no one else has considered?

---

1   Rosenshine, Principles of Instruction.

Of course, it isn't always possible to answer every question students may have in class without derailing the entire lesson and distracting from the explanation, thereby taxing students' attention.[2] Examples of these kinds of questions include:

♦ How does money work?

♦ How did some countries get to be so rich while others are so much poorer?

♦ If some countries can't grow enough food, why don't we just send them the food we waste?

These are excellent geographical questions, which cut to the heart of many topics, but answering them in class, or attempting to, can mean that you end up having a conversation with one student while the rest of the class wonder when you are going to get back on track. The easiest solution may be to explain that, while an excellent question, it is something that you would need to discuss in too much depth to go into now, but that you will either address it next lesson or find an alternative opportunity to talk to them about it. These are good examples of the fertile questions discussed previously: ones that could be asked at the end of a lesson to check that students have developed a deep understanding of the topic. It is worth making a note of these questions and checking at the end of the topic to see whether students can now answer them themselves.

As well as a creating a culture of asking questions, we also need to create one in which students feel comfortable answering them. The biggest barrier here is that students feel embarrassed by not knowing the answer. One way in which teachers deal with this is to rush on quickly and ask someone else; the problem with this being that the original student is left with the potential embarrassment of having not known the answer and of a peer being called on to help

---

2 For more on avoiding distractions in the lesson see: Peps Mccrea, *Memorable Teaching: Leveraging Memory to Build Deep and Durable Learning in the Classroom* (CreateSpace, 2017).

them out. A better solution may be to help them get to the right answer by prompting their memory. This might involve asking them a few more questions to scaffold their answer. For example, if you got an "I don't know" response to the question, "Why do you think Boscastle flooded?" you might follow it up with:

♦ What almost always happens before a river floods?

♦ Did people do anything that made the flood more likely?

♦ Do you remember last lesson when we looked at the map of the area? What was the landscape like?

♦ Think back to the point that Dan made about how they should have rebuilt the town somewhere else. Why did he think that?

Hopefully, the student you have asked should not only then be able to come up with an answer but will also have a better idea of the process involved in answering difficult questions, and will be able to draw on this in the future.

The rest of this chapter considers the strategies we can use in the classroom to ask good geographical questions.

1. Plan Your Questions

Do you know who you will ask what?

When planning a lesson, and in particular any explanations, it is worth spending some time thinking about the questions you want to ask. If you don't, there is always a risk that your questioning ends up in the kind of guessing game seen in Mr Johnson's classroom in the introduction to this chapter.

You might decide that you want to ask questions to relate what students are learning back to a previous topic. Doing so helps with the process of recall as well as enhancing their ability to make links between different parts of the subject. For example, before teaching a GCSE lesson about the Boscastle flood, you could ask the class to tell you about the physical and human factors that increase flood risk or even use a geological map of the area and ask questions to remind them of content covered previously at Key Stage 3. These kinds of questions need planning out in advance to allow you to prepare materials and prompts. In this way, we can see how questioning is intrinsically linked to effective explanation.

Another reason why it is important to plan out your questions is so you can consider the particular threshold concepts that students will encounter. Threshold concepts are bits of "troublesome knowledge" that can open up, or shut down, the topic.[3] They are things that, if not fully understood, can act as a barrier to students making further progress. We need to ask questions to establish who has understood them and to draw out any misconceptions.

An example of a threshold concept in geography is sustainability – and a common misconception is that it is only concerned with environmental issues. To explore this, you might ask a string of questions, such as:

♦ Sustainability ensures that the needs of the present day generation are met without harming what?

♦ Why might this mean that using coal-fired power stations isn't sustainable?

---

3 Meyer and Land, Threshold Concepts and Troublesome Knowledge.

♦ Does this mean that wind farms are always sustainable?

♦ Why might we argue that sustainability should be seen as a continuum rather than as an absolute?

This string of questions starts by covering the important definition of sustainability, without which nothing else makes sense. It then goes on to use the definition with a fairly straightforward example, before applying it to a more nuanced one that allows you to draw out points about economic considerations. The final question helps to develop students' deeper conceptual understanding of the subject. It tackles the issue of many students seeing environmental issues in binary terms of good and bad, whereas to think like geographers they need to see more shades of grey and draw conclusions with greater nuance.

As well as planning what to ask and why, we also need to consider how we are going to direct different questions. This is one reason why it is very important to know your class, as questioning allows you to address their specific strengths and weaknesses. In our sustainability example, we might ask the first question to someone who has struggled with the definition of sustainability before and tends to rush to answer a question without being clear on exactly what it is asking. We could then pose the second question to someone who we suspect may not have been listening to the answer of the first. The third could go to someone who usually thinks in very simple terms and the final one to someone who needs a challenge, before opening up the discussion to the class (see Strategy 5). By planning questions in advance, we can carefully consider their exact purpose and ensure that we ask the right type of question at the right time to the right student.

2. Go Off-Piste

When should you allow a question to take you off on a tangent?

Although lessons benefit from careful planning, we have to acknowledge the dynamic nature of the classroom. To put it in geographical terms, we have a range of inputs, information flows in unpredictable ways between different stores, and the potential outputs are numerous. This is a complex system. As such, we need to be prepared to go off-plan occasionally.

Sudden misconceptions

Questioning is a phase in a lesson when misconceptions are often revealed. Even questions about specific examples might expose deeper gaps in understanding. Questions about the advantages of London's location on the Thames might reveal that a distressing number of students still think that rivers begin at the sea. Questions on the impact of traffic congestion might reveal confusion around climate change and the hole in the ozone layer. Questions about Lagos might reveal misconceptions about economic development across Africa.

Without this underlying knowledge in place, it would be negligent to just continue with the planned lesson. Instead, we need to stop to address the area of confusion with a clear, albeit ad hoc, explanation and then provide the opportunity for students to practise using this new knowledge. It might be possible to link a task in which they use this information back to the intended aim of the lesson. For example:

♦ Explain why the banks of the Thames make a suitable location for a settlement *with reference to connections to the sea.*

♦ Give three problems caused by traffic congestion, *including how it contributes to global climate change.*

♦ Describe the quality of life in Lagos *by contrasting Makoko with Victoria Island.*

We need to have a deep well of knowledge to draw on and be well-practised at delivering clear and concise explanations before we can go off-plan and address misconceptions in this way.

Current events

One of the many reasons why geography is such an exciting subject is that it just keeps on happening. It is impossible to turn on the TV or to step outside without seeing something of geography-related interest, so it is not surprising that students come to our lessons wanting to ask us questions about the things that they have seen, whether this is a conflict somewhere in the world or a hurricane battering the Caribbean.

There are two ways of addressing this. The first would be to pause the curriculum and relate the lesson's content to what is happening in the news. The problem with this option is that the curriculum is planned in a certain way for a reason. It should, as Mary Myatt explains, tell a story and not just be one thing happening after another.[4] Stopping the curriculum to discuss a tropical storm in Haiti might be engaging, but if you haven't taught low-pressure systems, development indicators and issues around trade relationships, it will also be fairly meaningless as students won't have the prior knowledge on which to hook the information they are learning.

The second, and perhaps better, approach might be to sacrifice the final part of the lesson to discuss the world event that students want to know about. This could be an opportunity to show how it links to what they have learnt and, importantly, how it will link to future topics. This could also present a good opportunity to put together some information or resources that could be used by form tutors during morning registration to answer these questions and to keep geography at the forefront of students' minds.

---

4   Mary Myatt, Curriculum as a Big Story. Speech at researchEd Durrington, 28 April 2018.

3. Socratic Questions

How can we use different types of question to probe and develop understanding?

closed

socratic

Socratic questions are designed to challenge the accuracy and completeness of students' thinking about a topic. They move beyond the simple closed question and expected answer cycle – the one that didn't go according to plan in Mr Johnson's classroom in the introduction to this chapter – and towards a dialogic approach where questioning forms a full and important part of the learning process.[5]

Socratic questions are designed to achieve six different purposes, which I will outline shortly. We can use them in geography to take a short and simplistic answer to a complex question and use further questions and prompts to help students see and address this complexity. We can also use them to help students understand how to apply their knowledge to a question and how to generate new lines of enquiry.

---

5   Robin Alexander, *Towards Dialogic Teaching: Rethinking Classroom Talk*, 5th edn (York: Dialogos, 2017).

Below is a series of questions and answers that exemplify the six types of Socratic question discussed in *Making Every Lesson Count*.[6] After an initial closed question, we can see how the teacher uses follow-up questioning to achieve various purposes:

Teacher: Should London prioritise protecting its green space?

Student: Yes.

1. **Classify their thinking.**

   Teacher: What do you know about the need for green space in London?

   Student: It helps to prevent flooding as water can infiltrate into the soil. It also provides space for communities and tourists like it.

2. **Probe assumptions.**

   Teacher: What would change your answer about prioritising green space?

   Student: If there was another way to prevent flooding, or if something more dangerous than flooding would happen if not.

3. **Demand evidence.**

   Teacher: What evidence is there that cities need this green space to prevent flooding?

   Student: In Lagos, they built on open land in the city and flooding increased.

4. **Consider alternative viewpoints.**

   Teacher: Would everyone agree that green space should be a priority in cities?

   Student: No. If we don't build on this land then house prices will be more expensive. This might mean that people who can't afford a house would have different priorities.

---

6   Allison and Tharby, *Making Every Lesson Count*, pp. 207–209.

5. **Explore implications.**

    Teacher: What would be the implications of saying that London should prioritise green space?

    Student: It would mean that the authorities would need to act to protect green space and ban building on it. It might mean that developers need to look for somewhere else to put homes, like brownfield sites.

6. **Question the question.**

    Teacher: Why do you think we need to ask questions like this?

    Student: We can't prioritise everything and need to consider what we think is most important.

By the end of this process the student, and the class who have been listening to the exchange and have been encouraged to contribute, should be able to give a much more developed answer to any further questions about the challenges faced by urban areas and the potential solutions.

4. Hinge Questions

How can we find out whether students really understand?

One of the reasons why we ask students questions is to check that they understand what we have been explaining. The problem with asking ad hoc questions as they occur to us is that they may tell us very little about what has really been learnt. For example, after spending some time explaining the causes of the Boscastle flood we might ask, "What was the main reason why Boscastle flooded?" Answers might include:

"There was a lot of rain."

"The village was next to a river."

"The valley was really steep."

"Fallen trees blocked the bridges."

All of these are valid answers to the question but you would be hard pressed to really know who had understood what from these responses. This is where hinge questions come in. These are questions that are planned in advance to really check the depth of understanding in parts of the lesson that are critical to students moving on. The lesson "hinges" on these questions being answered, as there is no point pressing on if this essential content has not been mastered.

Hinge questions are often framed as multiple-choice questions, as the potential answers are carefully limited and can be chosen in a way that is actually very revealing. Daisy Christodoulou explains that multiple-choice questions are often dismissed as being too simple, but as long as all the potential answers appear plausible they can be fiendishly tricky.[7] She often uses the example of capital cities to demonstrate this. Try this one:

What is the capital of Tajikistan?

A. Bishkek

B. Astana

C. Dushanbe

D. Ashgabat

Unless you know your central Asian republics well, the answer is going to be difficult to guess. Compare it with:

What is the capital of Tajikistan?

A. London

---

7 Daisy Christodoulou, *Making Good Progress? The Future of Assessment for Learning* (Oxford: Oxford University Press, 2016), pp. 163–169.

B.   *Paris*

C.   *Dushanbe*

D.   *Rome*

Here you can see the importance of all the answers being plausible.

You can then use multiple choices to test misconceptions by including them as possible answers. For example:

Which of the following contribute to global warming?

A.   *burning fossil fuels*

B.   *methane*

C.   *the hole in the ozone layer*

D.   *deforestation*

E.   *the melting of ice*

Furthermore, note that this question has three correct answers but that the person answering doesn't know how many they need to find. They genuinely need to know the topic in order to identify the correct answers, rather than relying on the process of elimination.

You can also use multiple-choice questions with different correct answers to check the depth of students' understanding. For example:

Why did Boscastle flood? Pick the best correct answer:

A.   *There was heavy rain.*

B.   *The steep valley sides meant the lag time was short and the river couldn't contain the water.*

C.   *The river had been artificially straightened upstream.*

D. *Deforestation led to soil erosion that made the river chan-nel too shallow to contain the water.*

Both A and B are correct but b shows greater understand-ing. Both C and D are reasons why rivers flood but they don't apply in this case.

Planning in these kinds of hinge questions can be useful to quickly identify whether students have the understanding of the topic needed to proceed with the lesson, or whether an aspect might need reteaching or developing with a different follow-up activity.

5. Involving Everyone

What can we do to get everyone answering questions?

One potential problem with questioning is that it can lead to a situation in which a handful of students are engaging with the lesson, asking and answering questions and thinking hard, while the rest of the class daydream. If we aren't care-ful we can be led to believe that a whole class has fully understood a topic on the basis of just a couple of students answering questions that the rest of them wouldn't be able to. We need to find a way of involving everyone.

One strategy to help us achieve this is to select students to answer questions at random. In this way, we can hope to get a more representative sample of the class. Some teachers like to write students' names on lollipop sticks, others use ran-dom name generators on a computer or handheld electronic device; either way, the idea is to select a name without sub-conscious teacher bias. Furthermore, once students realise that they could be called upon to answer a question, they are more incentivised to pay close attention to what is being said, or to ask for clarification if something doesn't make sense. A problem with relying entirely on random questioning, however, is that it reduces your ability to target questions, the advantages of which we discussed previously. As with any strategy, you need to consider which approach will be best suited to what you are trying to achieve at that point in time.

Another way to involve more students in answering is to ask questions in way that allows mass participation. This could include:

- **The use of mini-whiteboards.** These work especially well for multiple-choice hinge questions as students can quickly record the letter linked to the answer. Just make sure that they all reveal the answer at the same time or you may find the class copying the first person to hold theirs up.

- **Using quiz apps.** There are a range of computer programs that allow you to set quizzes on a topic and collect students' responses. You can even use something like Google Docs to build up a spreadsheet of who knew what about each topic and use this to help students target gaps in their knowledge when it comes to revision.

- **Sticky notes.** Some students find it hard to overcome their shyness about coming forward with an answer in front of the class. You could ask each student to write the answer to a question on a sticky note and place it on the board. This works especially well for questions with answers that fit along a spectrum, to practise "to what extent" responses or when answers can be placed on a location. For example:

  ◊ Where would you place coal as a fuel source on a continuum from very sustainable to not-at-all sustainable?

  ◊ Where on this town plan should the new supermarket be built?

◊ Where on this sustainability Venn diagram would you put "farmland floods following a natural disaster"? Under economic, social or environmental impact or in an intersection?

Ask students to write their name on their sticky note so you can ask follow-up questions once they have had time to consider their response in light of the views of others.

6. Asking Geographical Questions

Can we get students to ask questions like a geographer?

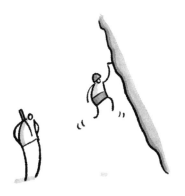

As I said at the start of this chapter, geography is a questioning discipline. We want our students to look at the world around them and ask questions. They should look at a landscape and ask:

♦ Why are the hills shaped in this way?

♦ How would this landscape have looked 50,000 years ago?

- What role does geology play in how people use this place?

- How are human actions shaping this landscape?

One barrier to students asking questions like these is a lack of knowledge about what such questions explore. To think to ask about the role of geology in shaping human action, you have to know that geology can have an effect on this. You probably need to have seen some examples of where this has happened before you would think to ask the question of a new place. So the first step in encouraging questioning is to equip students with the knowledge to explore and to interrogate, and to question with.

The next step in encouraging students to ask geographical questions is to model them. We can start a lesson by showing an image, a graph or a map and interrogating it in the way a geographer would. We can demonstrate the types of questions we might ask of our source and explain why we are asking them. What is it about this source that triggers these questions? How are we applying our prior knowledge to draw out information about this particular source?

Once the process has been modelled, we need to give students the opportunity to ask questions. As with anything else new, we will probably need to give them a scaffold. The most common method is to provide question stems that students can complete. For example:

- Where does the ...?

- How did the ...?

- Why are they ...?

- When would ...?

- Who might ...?

There is also an opportunity to do this when we pose fertile questions at the start of a topic. We might start with the problem, "Why was the construction of the Jubilee flood relief channel controversial?" and ask students to come up with the enquiry questions they would need to answer to respond to the question fully. If they are knowledgeable about issues around flooding and flood defences, they will hopefully come up with questions like:

◆ Where is the flood relief channel?

◆ Had the area previously flooded?

◆ Have there been any floods since?

◆ How much did it cost?

◆ Who were the stakeholders?

By forming these questions in advance, they are fashioning mental hooks for the information that they will receive and are creating links between what they already know about the issue and what they will learn. In this way, they are developing their schemata: those mental representations that shape understanding.

In this final case study, Laura Pellegrino shares how one questioning strategy has had a transformative effect on participation.

Case Study: Questioning

Laura Pellegrino, geography NQT, The Regis School

Once the headache of ensuring that every student has a working whiteboard pen is over, and the novelty of doodling passes, mini-whiteboards – or laminated card if you're feeling thrifty – are a staple questioning tool, for me at least. From multiple-choice questions to identify and quash misconceptions to the construction of definitions, whiteboards allow a quick and very visual check on understanding. Whereas verbal questioning – whether it be voluntary or targeted – allows the voices of a select few to be heard, whiteboards provide me as the teacher with access to all thirty voices in a class.

At the beginning of my training year, I found the prospect of questioning to be a minefield, unknowingly choosing the same select few students to answer every time I asked a question. This ultimately provided me with an inefficient and unrepresentative way of assessing the learning taking place within my classroom. However, the nature of mini-whiteboards as a whole-class approach encourages a high participation rate as it's easily accessible and allows thinking time.

A by-product of this questioning tool is the influence it has had on classroom confidence, an issue I personally found challenging to deal with at the beginning of my training. Whereas the verbally enthusiastic or high-attaining rush to put their hands up, and jitter in their seats looking like they're about to implode, for others the prospect of offering an answer to the class is daunting. I've found in several cases that the use of whiteboards encourages participation and increases students' comfort, by eliminating the fear that the whole class' attention will be drawn to individuals.

Final Thoughts: Theory into Practice

It is important that, as professionals, we understand why we make the decisions we do. It may be true that everything works somewhere, but some things are more likely to work in some places, and are likely to work better, than in others – either by being more effective, more efficient, or both. This book has attempted to address the question of what we need to do in the classroom to make sure that each lesson leads to students learning more, understanding the world better and developing their geographical skills. By looking at these aims in relation to each of the six principles, we can develop an understanding of the mechanism of a successful lesson. However, this also begs the question, what does it look like when we put it all together?

We want to avoid seeing the six principles as a checklist for a lesson and merely looking to demonstrate that we have included them all. They are likely to overlap and the lines between them will be blurry. When you are explaining a new concept, you will be questioning and modelling. You might also be providing feedback on the answers that students give to your questions or about misconceptions that they had last time they looked at this topic. When students are practising, they might also be reflecting on feedback you have given them, using your model and remembering your explanation and, hopefully, all of this will be based on challenge.

Another reason why we can't view these principles as a lesson-by-lesson checklist is because the idea of a lesson as a unit of time is inherently flawed. We are used to thinking of a lesson as a period of time, usually an hour, during which we meet an objective. This objective might be to explain the impact of unbalanced trading relationships on LICs, to describe the processes in the middle course of a river or to assess the effect of changing demographics on an urban area. What they all have in common is that each of these objectives will magically take exactly an hour to meet, unless you have fifty-minute lessons, in which case they will take that long.

The first step in applying the principles in this book in the classroom is to stop seeing lessons as blocks of time and instead consider them as part of a sequence of learning. Chunks within this sequence might take ten minutes – for example, explaining how an oxbow lake is formed – or five hours – for example, to unpick why Haiti's economic development has fallen behind the rest of the western hemisphere. Over the course of this sequence you will have set a challenge, explained the content, modelled what success looks like, given students practice tasks, questioned them and given feedback.

This conclusion looks at how we can bring the six principles together. First, we'll look at an example GCSE lesson that demonstrates how I go about combining the six principles in my classroom, then finally, we'll consider some wider implications for their implementation.

The Principles in Practice

This is a GCSE lesson looking at an example of a large-scale water transfer scheme. It builds towards answering the fertile question, "Who benefits most from the building of the Lesotho Highland Water Project (LHWP)?" and the sequence of learning runs for around three hours. The specification calls for students to know about an example of a water transfer scheme, but this scheme of work goes beyond that requirement by asking them to make quite a complex assessment of it.

Students are going to need to apply some knowledge about weather patterns, water security and development indicators, so we start with a quick quiz including questions on each of these topics. This will strengthen their recall of the information and provide a hook for what they are about to learn. It will signpost them to the pre-existing knowledge in their schema, their network of knowledge, allowing them to build on this. Here we can see the principles of *practice* and *questioning* in action.

As a prompt, they look at a photo of one of the dams built as part of the LHWP and I introduce the fertile question that they will go on to answer. I ask them to come up with the geographical questions they will need to explore first in order to develop a complete answer. My aim is to encourage them to think like geographers, using the skill and principle of *questioning*.

Next, we look at the location of the LHWP. I quickly remind them how to write a description of location, by *modelling*, and then ask them to give three pieces of information about where the project is located. I *question* them about why this is a good location for a dam based on several maps, prompting them to consider relief rainfall and population density in the area and then I *explain* the differences in development between Lesotho, where the water is captured, and South Africa, where it ends up. As I talk, I make a few notes about key facts on the whiteboard to support my *explanation*. Students can refer back to these to jog their working memory when they write their own explanation of why a water transfer scheme was built in this location: the *practice* task.

While the class are working, I look at the work of a few students who tend to struggle with extended writing and offer additional scaffolding where needed, meaning that all students are supported to rise to the *challenge*. I also see some good examples of explanation that I share with the class: *modelling* what I'm looking for as a form of *feedback*. They then make a few alterations to their work based on these examples; they engage in *practice*, acting on the *feedback*.

I then talk them through a few details of the scheme and show them different images to illustrate the key points, an *explanation* which uses the principles of dual coding. They watch a short video clip of the views of different stakeholders and read about the scheme in the textbook: both examples of *explanation* in a different format. As they read, they organise their notes into a table showing the advantages and disadvantages for South Africa and Lesotho and then colour-code them to identify economic, social and environmental issues.

They now have the background information and understanding in place to answer their fertile question. Before they start, I use *questioning* to draw out potential misconceptions – for example, around the issue of getting into debt to pay for the dams, why farmers in Lesotho might still need this stored water despite higher rainfall, and about the way in which dams operate. I also focus on the threshold concept of "sustainability" that is implicit in the question, providing *challenge*. Finally, I *model* the way in which I want them to write their answers by showing an exemplar about a different project. They can now answer the fertile question, "Who benefits most from the building of the Lesotho Highland Water Project (LHWP)?"

Once they have answered the question, I read through the students' work and make notes about the strengths and weaknesses, which I will use to give the whole class *feedback*. The students then look at their own work to identify these strengths and weaknesses and subsequently make corrections. While they are doing this, I talk to individual students who need more specific *feedback*.

By the end of this scheme of work, students will have:

♦ Refreshed their memory of relief rainfall, development indicators and water insecurity.

♦ Practised describing location.

♦ Practised asking geographical questions.

♦ Learnt the details of a particular water transfer scheme.

♦ Learnt how such schemes create winners and losers.

♦ Applied this example to the concept of sustainability – and so practised using it in a new context.

Making Every Geography Lesson Count: In the Curriculum

One thread that runs through all six principles in this book is the curriculum. The word originates from the Latin term describing the course of a race – the path from beginning to end – and each lesson in your curriculum should be a step forward in that race. This means that, to a great extent, your lesson is only going to be as good as your curriculum. If your course is plagued with obstacles, twists and turns, each step will be that bit harder.

There isn't the space in this book to fully explore how to create a geography curriculum that will ensure every lesson counts, and indeed every school will have their own ideas and specifications to incorporate, but here are a few questions to keep in mind:

♦ **What is important?** Geography is a vast subject and can be studied through all manner of topics: the geography of fashion, sport, crime or video games, for example. You name it, you could probably teach it. However, time is very limited so you need to decide what to include and what to omit. You need to decide what you feel really matters, and what will represent meaningful learning for your students in your school.

♦ **How should it be structured?** The varying nature of the subject can mean that it sometimes feels as though we are just moving from topic to topic in no particular order. A temptation is to structure the curriculum on an ad hoc basis to exploit students' interests. Perhaps something that students find particularly exciting occurs just as they are selecting their Year 9 options or lessons are adapted to tie in with a sporting fixture. I've seen teachers add in a topic on Russia just in time for the 2018 World Cup or on Brazil before the 2016 Olympics. While it makes sense to capture students' interests, instead, we need to consider the journey as a whole. What do they need to do in one topic so they can make sense of the next?

♦ **How can we interleave exam topics?** To a certain extent, our curricula at Key Stages 4 and 5 are determined by the exam board's syllabus. However, we don't need to see this as a to-do list to work through and tick off in order. You have a lot of freedom in terms of the places you choose to study and the examples you use. If you need to look at the challenges of water management, you could explore them in the country that you are using as an LIC case study and you could even use this same country to study the challenges of urban areas. You should be able to layer up different topics and find ways to interleave and revisit content in an engaging and meaningful way.

- ♦ **How can fieldwork support the work you do in class?** When planning your curriculum you may want to look for opportunities to use fieldwork to support what happens in the lesson. A lesson on microclimate will count all the more if students can investigate the microclimate around the school site. A study into the impact of globalisation will be all the more powerful if linked to their local high street.

The Gift of Geography

Geography is a hugely important school subject. We have the opportunity to pass on thousands of years of discoveries about how our world works and to equip students with the skills to add to these discoveries in the future. An education about our planet is our children's inheritance.

Studying geography shapes the way in which we see the world, and the chance to pass this on to the next generation is both an honour and a huge responsibility. As such, we need to make every geography lesson count.

Bibliography

Agarwal, Pooja K., Patrice M. Bain and Roger W. Chamberlain (2012). The Value of Applied Research: Retrieval Practice Improves Classroom Learning and Recommendations from a Teacher, a Principal and a Scientist, *Education Psychology Review* 24: 437–448.

Alexander, Robin (2017). *Towards Dialogic Teaching: Rethinking Classroom Talk*, 5th edn (York: Dialogos).

Allison, Shaun and Andy Tharby (2015). *Making Every Lesson Count: Six Principles to Support Great Teaching and Learning* (Carmarthen: Crown House Publishing).

Beck, Isabel L., Margaret G. McKeown and Linda Kucan (2002). *Bringing Words to Life* (New York: The Guilford Press).

Berger, Ron (2003). *An Ethic of Excellence: Building a Culture of Craftsmanship with Students* (Portsmouth, NH: Heinemann).

Berliner, David C., Pamela Stein, Donna Sabers, Pamela Brown Clarridge, Katherine Cushing and Stefinee Pinnegar (1988). Implications of Research on Pedagogical Expertise and Experience for Mathematics Teaching. In Douglas A. Grouws and Thomas J. Cooney (eds), *Perspectives on Research on Effective Mathematics Teaching* (Reston, VI: National Council of Teachers of Mathematics), pp. 67–95.

Chambers, Andrew (2009). Africa's Not-So-Magic Roundabout, *The Guardian* (24 November). Available at: https://www.theguardian.com/commentisfree/2009/nov/24/africa-charity-water-pumps-roundabouts.

Christodoulou, Daisy (2016). *Making Good Progress? The Future of Assessment for Learning* (Oxford: Oxford University Press).

Coe, Robert (2013). *Improving Education: A Triumph of Hope over Experience*, Inaugural Lecture of Professor Robert Coe, Durham University, 18 June. Available at: http://www.cem.org/attachments/publications/ImprovingEducation2013.pdf.

Coe, Robert, Cesare Aloisi, Steve Higgins and Lee Elliot Major (2014). *What Makes Great Teaching? Review of the Underpinning Research* (London: Sutton Trust). Available at: http://www.suttontrust.com/wp-content/uploads/2014/10/What-makes-great-teaching-FINAL-4.11.14.pdf.

Didau, David (2016). Are Teachers Cursed with Knowledge? *The Learning Spy* [blog] (5 September). Available at: http://www.learningspy.co.uk/featured/teachers-cursed-knowledge/.

Dunlosky, John (2013). Strengthening the Student Toolbox: Study Strategies to Boost Learning, *American Educator* 37(3): 12–21. Available at: https://www.aft.org/sites/default/files/periodicals/dunlosky.pdf.

Enser, Mark (2017). Model Live, *Heathfield Teach Share Blog* [blog] (9 January). Available at: https://heathfieldteachshare.wordpress.com/2017/01/09/model-live/.

Enser, Mark (2018). Teach Like Nobody's Watching, *Teaching It Real* [blog] (12 September). Available at: https://teachreal.wordpress.com/2018/09/12/teach-like-nobodys-watching-2/.

Ericsson, K. Anders, Ralf Th. Krampe and Clemens Tesch-Romer (1993). The Role of Deliberate Practice in the Acquisition of Expert Performance, *Psychological Review* 100(3): 363–406.

Gerhardt, Kurt (2010). Why Development Aid for Africa Has Failed, *Spiegel Online* (16 August). Available at: http://www.spiegel.de/international/world/time-for-a-rethink-why-development-aid-for-africa-has-failed-a-712068.html.

Hattie, John and Helen Timperley (2007). The Power of Feedback, *Review of Educational Research* 77(1): 81–112. Available at: http://education.qld.gov.au/staff/development/performance/resources/readings/power-feedback.pdf.

Hawley, Duncan (2018). On Shaky Ground: The Physical Facts of Recent Earthquake Events in Mexico, *Teaching Geography* 48(1): 32–35.

Jones, Emma (2018). Cone of Experience by Edgar Dale, *E-Learning Network* [blog] (8 February). Available at: http://resources.eln.io/experiences-cone-dale/.

Kirschner, Paul A., John Sweller and Richard E. Clark (2006). Why Minimal Guidance during Instruction Does Not Work: An Analysis of the Failure of Constructivist, Discovery, Project-Based, Experiential, and Inquiry-Based Teaching, *Educational Psychologist* 41(2): 75–86.

Knight, Oliver and David Benson (2014). *Creating Outstanding Classrooms: A Whole-School Approach* (Abingdon: Routledge).

Kuepper-Tetzel, Carolina (2018). Optimizing Your Learning Schedule, *The Learning Scientists* [blog] (5 July). Available at: http://www.learningscientists.org/blog/2018/7/5-1?rq=Ebbinghaus.

Lambert, David and John Morgan (2010). *Teaching Geography 11–18: A Conceptual Approach* (Maidenhead: Open University Press).

Mccrea, Peps (2017). *Memorable Teaching: Leveraging Memory to Build Deep and Durable Learning in the Classroom* (CreateSpace).

Marking Policy Review Group (2016). *Eliminating Unnecessary Workload Around Marking: Report of the Independent Teacher Workload Review Group* (London: Department for Education). Available at: https://www.gov.uk/government/publications/reducing-teacher-workload-marking-policy-review-group-report.

Mayer, Richard E. and Richard B. Anderson (1991). Animations Need Narrations: An Experimental Test of a Dual-Coding Hypothesis, *Journal of Educational Psychology* 83(4): 484–490.

Meyer, Jan H. F. and Ray Land (2003). Threshold Concepts and Troublesome Knowledge: Linkages to Ways of Thinking and Practising within the Disciplines. In Chris Rust (ed.), *Improving Student Learning: Theory and Practice Ten Years On* (Oxford: Oxford Centre for Staff and Learning Development), pp. 412–424.

Myatt, Mary (2018). Curriculum as a Big Story. Speech at researchEd Durrington, 28 April.

Newmark, Ben (2017). Ten principles for Great Explicit Teaching, *BENNEWMARK* [blog] (7 October). Available at: https://bennewmark. wordpress.com/2017/10/07/ten-principles-for-great-explict-teaching/.

Ofsted (2015). *Key Stage 3: The Wasted Years?* Reference no: 150106 (September). Available at: https://www.gov.uk/government/ publications/key-stage-3-the-wasted-years.

Quigley, Alex (2016). *The Confident Teacher: Developing Successful Habits of Mind, Body and Pedagogy* (Abingdon: Routledge).

Quigley, Alex and Eleanor Stringer (2018). Making Sense of Metacognition, *Impact: Journal of the Chartered College of Teaching* 3: 26–30. Available at: https://impact.chartered.college/article/ quigley-stringer-making-sense-metacognition/.

Roberts, Margaret (2013). *Geography through Enquiry: Approaches to Teaching and Learning in the Secondary School* (Sheffield: Geographical Association).

Roberts, Margaret (2017). Planning for Enquiry. In Mark Jones (ed.), *The Handbook of Secondary Geography* (Sheffield: The Geographical Association), pp. 48–60.

Roche, Fergal (2017). *Mining for Gold: Stories of Effective Teachers* (Woodbridge: John Catt Educational).

Roediger, Henry L. and Andrew C. Butler (2011). The Critical Role of Retrieval Practice in Long-Term Retention, *Trends in Cognitive Sciences* 15(1): 20–27.

Roediger, Henry L. and Jeffrey D. Karpicke (2006). Test-Enhanced Learning: Taking Memory Tests Improves Long-Term Retention, *Psychological Science* 17(3): 249–255. Available at: https://www.ncbi.nlm. nih.gov/pubmed/16507066.

Rosenshine, Barak (2012). Principles of Instruction: Research-Based Strategies That All Teachers Should Know, *American Educator* 36(1): 12–19, 39. Available at: https://www.aft.org/sites/default/files/ periodicals/Rosenshine.pdf.

Standish, Alex (2018). The Place of Regional Geography. In Mark Jones and David Lambert (eds), *Debates in Geography Education*, 2nd edn (Abingdon: Routledge), pp. 62–74.

Storm, Benjamin C., Robert A. Bjork and Jennifer C. Storm (2010). Optimizing Retrieval as a Learning Event: When and Why Expanding

Retrieval Practice Enhances Long-Term Retention, *Memory and Cognition* 38(2): 244–253.

Taylor, Liz (2017). Progression. In Mark Jones (ed.), *The Handbook of Secondary Geography* (Sheffield: Geographical Association), pp. 40–47.

Thom, Jamie (2018). *Slow Teaching: On Finding Calm, Clarity and Impact in the Classroom* (Woodbridge: John Catt Educational).

Wiliam, Dylan (2017). Assessment, Marking and Feedback. In Carl Hendrick and Robin MacPherson, *What Does This Look Like in the Classroom? Bridging the Gap Between Research and Practice* (Woodbridge: John Catt Educational), pp. 27–44.

Willingham, Daniel T. (2009). *Why Don't Students Like School? A Cognitive Scientist Answers Questions About How the Mind Works and What It Means for the Classroom* (San Francisco, CA: Jossey-Bass).

Making Every Lesson Count

Six principles to support great teaching and learning

Shaun Allison and Andy Tharby

ISBN: 978-184590973-4

This award-winning title has now inspired a whole series of books. Each of the books in the series are held together by six pedagogical principles – challenge, explanation, modelling, practice, feedback and questioning – and provide simple, realistic strategies that teachers can use to develop the teaching and learning in their classrooms.

A toolkit of techniques that teachers can use every lesson to make that lesson count. No gimmicky teaching – just high-impact and focused teaching that results in great learning, every lesson, every day.

Suitable for all teachers – including trainee teachers, NQTs and experienced teachers – who want quick and easy ways to enhance their practice.

ERA Educational Book Award winner 2016. Judges' comments: "A highly practical and interesting resource with loads of information and uses to support and inspire teachers of all levels of experience. An essential staffroom book."

Making every
science
lesson count

Six principles to support
great science teaching

Shaun Allison

Making Every Science Lesson Count

Six principles to support great science teaching

Shaun Allison

ISBN: 978-178583182-9

Making Every Science Lesson Count goes in search of answers to the fundamental question that all science teachers must ask: "What can I do to help my students become the scientists of the future?"

Shaun points a sceptical finger at the fashions and myths that have pervaded science teaching over the past decade or so and presents a range of tools and techniques that will help science teachers make abstract ideas more concrete and practical demonstrations more meaningful.

Making every
English
lesson count

Six principles to support
great reading and writing

Andy Tharby

Making Every English Lesson Count

Six principles to support great reading and writing

Andy Tharby

ISBN: 978-178583179-9

Brings the teaching of conceptual knowledge, vocabulary and challenging literature to the foreground and shows teachers how to develop students' reading and writing proficiency over time.

Andy taps into the transformational effect that quality English teaching can have, and talks secondary school English teachers through effective methods that will challenge students to read and think beyond the confines of their world.

Making Every Primary Lesson Count

Six principles to support great teaching and learning

Jo Payne and Mel Scott

ISBN: 978-178583181-2

Shares a host of strategies designed to cultivate a growth mindset in the primary school classroom and guide children towards independence: motivating both teachers and pupils to aim high and put in the effort required to be successful in all subject areas.

Jo and Mel also offer tips on how to implement effective routines and procedures so that students are clear about what is expected from them.

Making Every Maths Lesson Count

Six principles to support great maths teaching

Emma McCrea

ISBN: 978-178583332-8

Making Every Maths Lesson Count provides practical solutions to perennial problems and inspires a rich, challenging and evidence-based approach to secondary school maths teaching.

Emma shares gimmick-free advice that combines the time-honoured wisdom of excellent maths teachers with the most useful evidence from cognitive science – enabling educators to improve their students' conceptual understanding of maths over time.

Making every
MFL
lesson count

*Six principles to support
great foreign language teaching*

James A. Maxwell
Edited by Shaun Allison and Andy Tharby

Making Every MFL Lesson Count

Six principles to support great foreign language teaching

James A. Maxwell

ISBN: 978-178583396-0

Making Every MFL Lesson Count equips modern foreign language (MFL) teachers with practical techniques designed to enhance their students' linguistic awareness and to help them transfer the target language into long-term memory.

Written for new and experienced practitioners alike, *Making Every MFL Lesson Count* skilfully marries evidence-based practice with collective experience and, in doing so, inspires a challenging approach to secondary school MFL teaching.

Making every
history
lesson count

*Six principles to support
great history teaching*

Chris Runeckles
Edited by Shaun Allison and Andy Tharby

Making Every History Lesson Count

Six principles to support great history teaching

Chris Runeckles

ISBN: 978-178583336-6

Writing in the practical, engaging style of the award-winning *Making Every Lesson Count*, Chris Runeckles articulates the fundamentals of great history teaching and shares simple, realistic strategies designed to deliver memorable lessons.

The book is underpinned by six pedagogical principles – challenge, explanation, modelling, practice, feedback and questioning – and equips history teachers with the tools and techniques to help students better engage with the subject matter and develop more sophisticated historical analysis and arguments.